raw

lovingly dedicated to
natasha blankfield

you truly inspire me
with your creativity & originality

# raw

## 150 dairy-free
## and gluten-free
## vegan recipes

omid jaffari

botanical cuisine

MURDOCH BOOKS

Kitchens are where I have spent most of my life. My grandmother's kitchen in Iran is the birthplace of my identity - it is where everything I know about myself was formed.

My earliest memories are of stealing cherries and pomegranates from my grandmother's backyard, before they were fully ripe. She had a cherry tree and a pomegranate tree, and we were not allowed to eat the pomegranates inside the house, because the juice would go everywhere, but the juice of the pomegranate is the best thing I have ever tasted in my life. I still love to cook with sour, half-ripened cherries and pomegranates, of course, with rosewater. I remember these massive tall garden walls with big Mohammadi roses tumbling everywhere. Their smell is unforgettable. No other rose smells as good as that. Once you have smelled these roses you can understand why Iranians use rosewater in everything. In Iran, all the mosques are washed with Mohammadi rosewater and there's rosewater in all our desserts, and even our savoury dishes. My mum would also wash the floors with rosewater, and I do the same.

I was born in Iran in 1979. My memories of my early childhood revolve around the kitchen and garden of my grandmother's house in northern Tehran, where I lived with my family. During the turbulent years of the Iranian revolution of 1979 and the subsequent war with Iraq, my family experienced great difficulties. My father, a recognised film director and actor, was seen as a traitor to Islam due to his film work and we were forced to flee Iran when I was seven years old. First we fled to Turkey for almost three years, then spent another two years in Malaysia before settling down in New Zealand as political refugees in February 1992.

When I was eighteen years old, I started working in Richard Ransfield's kitchen at Café 98 in Auckland. It was here that I truly began to understand the significance of our relationship with food. It taught me the importance of technique, structure and the value of the classic Western repertoire. Until then, nothing had ever tasted quite as good as my mother's food. I then moved to Auckland's harbourside café Viaduct and worked my way up from deep-fry chef to executive cold larder chef within nine months. This was during the hectic time of New Zealand's America's Cup victory in 2000. What a steep and wonderful learning curve!

But moving from place to place as a child must have fuelled in me an intense desire to learn more about culinary traditions around the globe, so I then spent more than a decade travelling in Asia, the Middle East, Africa, Europe and South America.

In the UK in 2002, I was lucky enough to work with Ruth Watson at the Crown and Castle Hotel in Orford, Suffolk. Here I experienced first-hand how food presentation and modern fusion cooking could be elevated to a whole new level, using only the freshest of fresh ingredients. It was Ruth who encouraged me to trust in my palate and who gave me the confidence to call myself a chef.

Then, a stint at the world-renowned River Café with Ruth Rogers and Rose Gray set me on the food journey that was to culminate in botanical cuisine. All these experiences helped hone my palate and my skills, and opened my mind to the possibilities of re-imagining raw cuisine.

In early 2010, I arrived in Australia from Japan, ready for a new culinary adventure - one that nourishes, helps nature, is economically sustainable and for the most part easily accessible. The journey evolved from conducting culinary educational tours around Australia during 2011 to manufacturing a sustainable organic raw vegan range of products.

Today, I am the managing director of the Melbourne-based business botanical cuisine. We pride ourselves on making simple, nutrient-dense products in small batches, using only the freshest, ethically sourced organic ingredients available to us. Our products are free from dairy, gluten, sugar, soy and preservatives, and the range is made at low temperatures, with minimal processing, no artificial additives and using sustainable methods. (For the home kitchen and greater convenience, soy-based miso and tamari may be used.) As a means to teach these skills, I founded the botanical cuisine academy. The culinary arts never stop evolving; they break new boundaries and unveil new standards for creativity and excellence.

Imbued with a passion for health and humanity, my goal is to inspire others to work towards a better, cleaner, animal cruelty-free world.

botanical cuisine

contents

the book

Making this book wasn't about promoting the health benefits of plant-based cuisine, as that is a given. Rather, its goal is to give you the tools to create a structured, functional kitchen, and to inspire good habits using the following elements: an organised kitchen, carefully chosen raw materials and lovingly prepared staples. Combining these elements allows you to create simple, clean, beautiful recipes every time.

I'd like to tell you that everything in this book is fast and easy to make, but I'd be lying. As my mother always said, there is nothing that can be fast, easy and also taste good. Otherwise, she would have a happy marriage. I am still bewildered by the marriage metaphor, but I do believe that delicious, wholesome food takes time – and choosing the right produce with care is incredibly important, whether it's plucked from your home garden, bought from a farmers' market or health food store, or selected from the organic section of your local supermarket. With increased awareness of the many health benefits of organic foods, it has become much easier to buy organic, biodynamic, pesticide-free produce. With a bit of guidance, a clutter-free kitchen, the right tools, premium raw materials and a good handful of love and patience, you can enjoy creating honest, good food that feeds the soul and nourishes the body.

To me, raw food genuinely is slow food. Think about it – when it takes 24 hours to prepare jam rather than 8 hours, which batch is receiving the most love and attention? Cooking food slowly preserves and enhances its natural attributes, creating rich flavours and textures.

I have written this book to share some building blocks for creating everyday raw vegan cuisine. (These form the backbone of botanical cuisine academy's raw vegan short courses.) Essentially, they reflect my personal commitment to creating food that fully respects mother nature and everything that she has given us. Above anything else, this book is about the joy of food, and learning to make exciting and inspirational dishes from nature.

# WHAT IS RAW AND VEGAN?

## RAW

In a nutshell, raw means that no food is heated above 45°C (113°F), thereby retaining more nutrients and enzymes than cooked food. A raw food diet involves eating live, nutritionally dense, uncooked, unprocessed and preferably organic foods or wild foods to ensure optimum health and wellbeing.

It's not always possible to maintain a 100% raw diet. While the majority of the recipes in this book can accurately be described as raw cuisine, there are a few ingredients that are not strictly so - freshly brewed coffee, for example. If you want to follow a strict 100% raw dietary path, avoid these particular recipes or substitute raw ingredients. There are still plenty of ideas that will suit your level of dedication.

## VEGAN

Veganism is a philosophy as well as a food choice. Vegans promote an animal product-free, sustainable, ethical and cleaner lifestyle. Most people find that adopting a vegan diet vastly improves their health because there is significantly less stress on the digestive system. However, choosing a raw food lifestyle must be a gradual process, changing our eating habits slowly by adding organic raw vegan meals into our daily routine. Always add, so you don't feel you are taking away or going without. Also, remember to consider everything in moderation!

## DAIRY-FREE

Dairy has been linked to some allergies, skin conditions such as eczema, rosacea and acne, excessive mucus and inflammation. By omitting dairy from the diet and finding different sources of protein and calcium, many sufferers have found that their symptoms have lessened and their general health has improved. About 75% of the world's population are lactose intolerant in some way, though in countries where dairy has been historically consumed in large quantities (such as in Northern Europe), the numbers are much lower.

## GLUTEN-FREE

Gluten is a protein found in many grains such as wheat, rye, spelt and oats. Those with Coeliac disease or other forms of gluten intolerance need to cut gluten entirely from their diet to avoid symptoms such as abdominal pain, bloating and fatigue. Some believe that the increase in gluten intolerances is due to the over-consumption of many grains and grain products in Western society (cereal for breakfast, sandwich for lunch, cake for afternoon tea, pasta for dinner). Others blame the changing nature of grains in modern farming practices, such as wheat hybridisation. Others point to the fact that more people are relying on heavily processed foods with high levels of gluten, such as pasta and bread. What is known is that a gluten-free diet can vastly improve a sufferer's digestion, general health and wellbeing.

## SUGAR-FREE

Sugar is addictive, and study after study has proven this. The more processed and refined the sugar is, the more detrimental the health effects. It's not surprising that many health experts call sugar a poison. It has been linked to tooth decay, obesity, diabetes and heart disease. Natural sweeteners are readily available these days and are much better alternatives – with far fewer side effects.

## LOW GI

GI stands for glycaemic index; it is a measure of the effects of carbohydrates in food on blood sugar levels. Foods with carbohydrates that break down quickly during digestion and release glucose rapidly into the bloodstream tend to have a high GI. Foods with carbohydrates that break down more slowly, releasing glucose more gradually into the bloodstream, tend to have a low GI. Foods that have a low GI can be a better choice for most people as they cause fewer spikes in blood sugar, resulting in a much steadier release of energy throughout the day.

## DEHYDRATION

The dehydrating process is a preserving technique that allows fruit, vegetables and other produce to be dried and stored, retaining most of their flavour, colour and nutritional value. Dehydration techniques have been used in recipes throughout this book to ensure minimal nutrient loss. These recipes have been tested using a domestic dehydrator. Note that dehydration times may differ, depending on the type of dehydrator used, humidity levels and the climate in which you're preparing meals (dehydration will be faster in warmer climes, while colder kitchens will require longer dehydration times). Make sure you test your ingredients for the ideal consistency before removing from the dehydrator.

## HIGH-SPEED BLENDING

A high-speed blender that runs at 1200-1500 watts is another important piece of equipment in the raw food kitchen. High-speed blenders will give far superior results when preparing raw food, helping to make textures smoother, lighter and more appealing, and also breaking down the fruits, vegetables, nuts and seeds in such a way that it's much easier for the body to absorb the vitamins, minerals and other nutrients. High extraction with shorter blending times also ensures lighter, less-compressed results.

raw materials

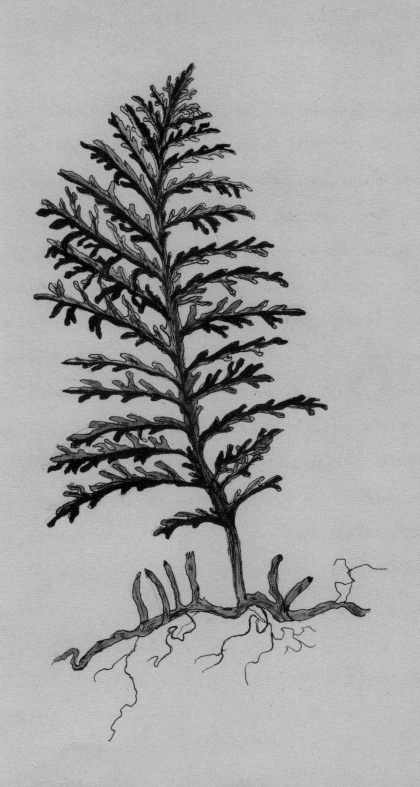

# INTRODUCTION TO RAW MATERIALS

These are the basic materials that will help you create everything from rustic everyday dishes to fine cuisine. All the ingredients you'll find in the raw material section are those we use every day at botanical cuisine to create our product range. You will find these ingredients are used many times, in many different ways. Once you get the hang of it, you'll know what a certain ingredient can do and you can start to play around with your own ideas, too!

# HOW TO USE YOUR KITCHEN TOOLS

Tools that I have listed in this section are, to a large extent, self-explanatory.

A 20 cm (8 in) vegetable knife is a great size to handle cutting all of your salad vegetables. A paring knife is ideal for your smaller produce, such as oranges, limes and strawberries. A palette knife can help you when working with desserts.

Zesters are great to use on your citrus for salads and marmalades. Use your fine grater for ginger and garlic.

Use silicone equipment, such as spatulas and whisks, because they last longer and, unlike metal equipment, they don't scratch or damage the metal bowls.

Use baking paper and masking tape (or elastic bands) when fermenting cashew - the paper is to cover and the tape (or elastic bands) is to hold the paper in place.

## TOOLS

20 cm (8 in) vegetable
  knife
Paring knife
Palette knife
Potato peeler
Julienne peeler
Zester
Fine grater or ginger grater
Chopping board
8 cm (3¼ in) pastry rings
  (stainless steel)
Measuring cups
Measuring spoons
Small spatula (silicone)
Small whisk (silicone)
Baking trays (stainless steel)
Deep baking trays
  (stainless steel)
Wire cooling rack
Baking paper
Masking tape
Small, medium and
  large mixing bowls
  (stainless steel)
Fine sieve
Muslin (cheesecloth)
Domestic dehydrator
Food processor
High-speed blender

## SHELF

Cold-pressed extra virgin
  olive oil
Sesame oil
Apple cider vinegar
Light agave syrup
Coconut nectar
Tamari
Cointreau
Brandy
Port
Rum
Food-grade essences
  such as mint

## FRIDGE

Cacao butter
Cold-pressed extra virgin
  coconut oil
Miso
Black olives
Spirulina
Vegan probiotics
Vanilla beans
Sunflower lecithin
Fresh produce
Fresh truffles, if the
  budget allows!

## NUTS & SPICES

Cashews
Walnuts
Cacao powder
Cacao nibs
Mesquite powder
Lucuma powder
Pink lake salt
Black pepper
Saffron
Cardamom pods
Cinnamon sticks
Coconut sugar
Fennel seeds
Coriander seeds
Pepperberries
Coffee beans
Guar gum

# GLOSSARY

## BIODYNAMIC

Biodynamic refers to the style of organic farming that incorporates practices that are in sync with the natural order.

## CACAO BEANS

A dried and fully fermented fatty seed (from the genus *Theobroma*), the cacao bean grows on a tree. The bean-like seeds are used in various forms: nibs, powder, butter and chocolate.

## CACAO BUTTER

Also called 'theobroma' oil, this is a pale-yellow edible vegetable fat extracted from the cacao bean. It's used as a thickening agent, and to give desserts a lovely glistening look. It also enhances the smell and flavour of various ingredients.

## CACAO NIBS

The 'nibs' are crushed beans. They are both crunchy and tender - a unique texture.

## CACAO POWDER

The powder from the cacao bean is used to make beautiful chocolates and bases for different earthy desserts.

## CAROB BEAN GUM (LOCUST BEAN GUM)

A thickening agent and gelling agent, carob bean gum is extracted from the seed of the carob tree.

## CASHEWS (RAW)

Cashews are nuts that are favoured for their flavour in raw food. Cashews have been used extensively in the recipes, forming the base of many dairy alternatives. Measurements in this book are for broken cashews. Although measurements for whole cashews may differ slightly, they won't affect the end result.

## CHOCOLATE LIQUOR

Chocolate liquor is solid, unsweetened baking chocolate. A chocolate mill or, more traditionally, a stone mill grinds and heats the cacao beans to make the chocolate liquor.

## COCONUT NECTAR

Coconut nectar has about 15 different amino acids, and is very good for you. It's very light and delivers sweetness, but not too much. It's a lovely combination of salt and sweet, and has a lovely texture.

## COCONUT SUGAR

Also known as coconut palm sugar, this cane sugar alternative is produced from the sap of the cut flower buds of the coconut palm. It is organic and sustainable, and has a naturally low GI rating.

## COLD-PRESSED EXTRA VIRGIN COCONUT OIL

Used as a setting agent, and for flavour and aroma, coconut oil is often included in desserts. We only use coconut oil with minimal processing, which has been extracted using a wet method centrifuge extraction process. This ensures its smoothness, lightness and maximum nutritional content.

## GUAR GUM

Also called 'guaram', this vegetable gum extract is used as a natural thickening agent, and is predominantly used in desserts. The off-white powder is, essentially, ground guar beans.

## ICE-CREAM/SORBET MAKER

This is a machine that churns ice-cream and sorbets. Alternatively, to save you buying more equipment, churning can be done with similar results in a food processor.

## LIGHT AGAVE NECTAR

Agave comes from a large, spiky plant that looks very similar to cactus or yuccas. The sap is extracted from the pina, the core of the plant, then filtered and heated at a low temperature, which breaks down the carbohydrates into sugar.

## LUCUMA POWDER

Lucuma is a South American fruit and the powder is derived from the dried, pulverised fruit. It is an excellent source of carbohydrates, fibre, vitamins and minerals. It smells woody and has a creamy citrus flavour.

## MESQUITE POWDER

Also known as algarroba, the seeds of this leguminous plant are harvested, dried and ground into flour. It has a beautiful caramel and vanilla flavour, and is used in our dessert section.

## MICRO SHISO

From the mint family, micro shiso has small reddish purple leaves, and is used in salads and desserts.

## MISO

Miso is a traditional Japanese food made from soya beans, rice and sea salt. These ingredients are mixed in various ratios and then fermented to create a wide variety of miso. For a soy-free alternative, you could try miso made from chickpeas, adzuki beans or brown rice.

## NETTLE LEAVES

There are more than 500 species of nettle grown worldwide. Though they are often mistaken for a weed, and can give you a very nasty sting, they are known to have numerous medicinal properties, and are especially high in iron. Once blanched slightly, nettles take on a beautiful pine nut and cinnamon flavour, and 'the sting' is removed.

## ORGANIC

Organic foods are those that are produced or grown without the use of pesticides, chemical fertilisers or other artificial chemicals. Organic foods tend to be mineral-rich, and support and nourish soil building and conservation.

## OYSTER MUSHROOMS

A common edible mushroom, the oyster mushroom has a reputation for being medicinally supportive and helping to reduce cholesterol. It has a bittersweet aroma (like anise or almonds) and is found in our dehydrated vegetable section.

## PEPPERBERRIES

*Tasmannia lanceolata*, also known as Cornish pepperleaf, is native to southeastern Australia. Spicy and fragrant, it has a strong pepper kick.

## PINK LAKE SALT

There's a large pink salt lake located in western Victoria in Australia, which is fed by natural salt aquifers. Each summer the lake dries to reveal a bed of salmon pink salt. A small amount of this salt is harvested annually by hand by the traditional owners of the land, and some of it makes its way into botanical cuisine products. The many rich qualities of the salt provide a complex well-rounded flavour.

## SEA SPRAY

Sea spray (also known as sea blite) is a herb with long thin fleshy leaves, which add a pleasant salty flavour to salads and other dishes.

## SPIRULINA POWDER

Known for its health-boosting qualities, spirulina powder is derived from an algae that is highly rich in protein and minerals. We use it for its unique earthy flavour.

## SUNFLOWER LECITHIN

An emulsifier that endows foods with a creamy, moist, smooth texture, sunflower lecithin is often used in chocolates, faux butters and baked goods. This fatty substance is obtained by dehydrating a sunflower seed and separating it into three parts: the oil, gum and other solids. Lecithin comes from the gum byproduct of this mechanical process.

## TAMARI

A gluten-free soy sauce with sweet, savoury and salty full-bodied flavour, tamari is derived from fermented soya beans and has little or no wheat. It is beautiful in mushroom-based recipes. For a soy-free alternative, you could try coconut aminos instead.

## TRUFFLES

Normally grown among the roots of trees, truffles are a highly prized subterranean fungi. They are beautiful in earthy flavoured recipes or to balance acidic or sweet notes.

## VEGAN PROBIOTICS (DAIRY-FREE)

Vegan probiotics are dairy free and contain bacterial cultures of *L. acidophilus* and other healthy bacteria. Prebiotics and probiotics are considered a positive way to improve digestive and immune system health. Probiotics are live sensitive cultures that need to be stored at 0-4°C (32-39°F).

## YOUNG THAI COCONUT MEAT

The flesh from a young Thai coconut is much softer and creamier than a mature coconut, and is ideal for drinks and desserts. It is sweet and delicious, low in fat and high in antioxidants.

## YOUNG THAI COCONUT WATER

The water of coconuts is dense with nutrients and easily absorbed by the body. Used widely in raw, plant-based cuisine, coconut water has many uses both technically and for health. Young Thai coconuts are particularly sweet.

35

37

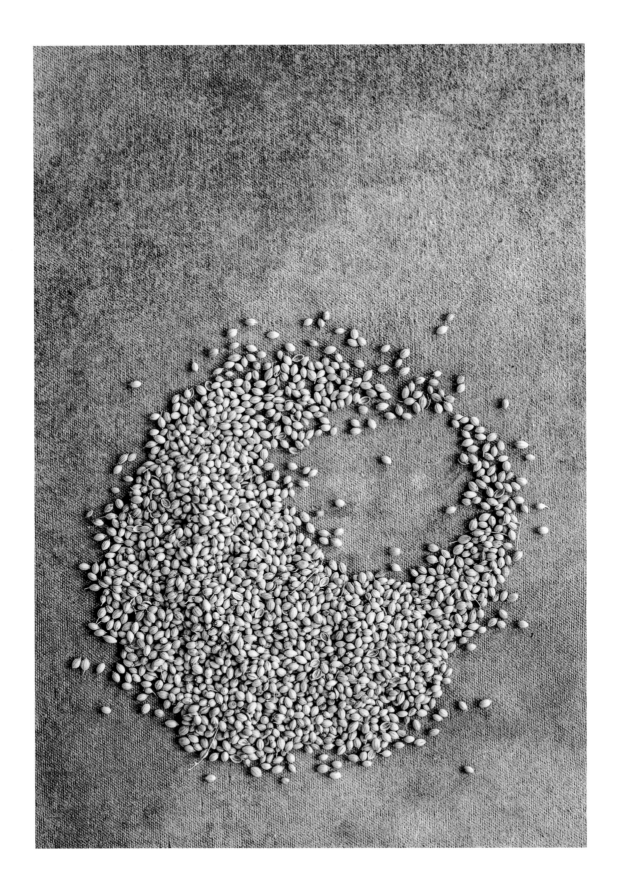

staples

# INTRODUCTION TO STAPLES

This section is designed for you to come back to, time and again. It's here that you'll learn the fundamentals of raw cuisine. Most of the recipes in this book start out using the basics from the staples section. You will start to see a pattern in the recipes. Every recipe has the same logic, and the staples can be mixed and matched to create everything from breakfasts to salads, from soups to chocolate.

You'll soon see that raw food isn't time-consuming when it comes to putting together your meals, but preparing the staples does take time! If you prepare your staples in advance, it becomes very simple to assemble and present a beautiful meal in no time at all. It just takes a little planning. Once you have your staples (dehydrated vegetables, pastry, pâtés, salts and sprinkles, infused sweeteners, cashew dairy, dressings, sauces and preserves) in the fridge or pantry, they're ready to use in your dishes whenever you need them. You can consistently create delicious honest food just by being a little organised.

That said, don't panic if you get caught short! You can buy suitable products from your farmers market or health food store, or even supermarkets with a big organic product section. Just buy the product that's as close as possible to the homemade version. Above all else, food should be fun and preparing it should not be a chore.

# NOTES ON THE RECIPES

## INGREDIENTS

- Use either filtered, rain, stream or mineral water for all recipes.
- Choosing produce to make jam, marmalade and dehydrated baby vegetables is completely up to you and what you have available. Simply choose seasonal and local, and it will naturally taste great.
- Prepare your produce before you start the recipe - wash the vegetables, peel the onions and garlic, etc.
- All coconut oils, cacao butters or cacao liquors need to be melted before use. To melt, place the required amount in a small bowl and sit it in the dehydrator set at 45°C (115°F) for 30 minutes, or fill the sink with hot water and allow the bowl to gently float on the water so the oils, butters or liquors can melt slowly.
- Always grate garlic cloves, ginger or French shallots when blending or putting in a food processor unless stated otherwise.
- Ideally, all spices should be freshly ground.

## VARIATIONS

- Always make sure to adjust the seasoning to your own taste if the stated seasoning does not please your palate.

## DEHYDRATION

- When dehydrating anything, it is best to use baking paper instead of silicone sheets so that the produce can breathe while dehydrating.
- During the dehydration process, we sometimes use baking paper to cover the produce on the baking trays so that they can dehydrate consistently. When covering with baking paper, ensure you place either spoons or something heavy on the baking paper so that the fan of the dehydrator does not lift the paper.

## CASHEW DAIRY

- In the recipes, I don't soak nuts to activate the enzymes unless specified. In all fermented methods, there is no need to soak nuts as they will be soaking with water and probiotics, which will naturally activate them.
- When fermenting cashew yoghurt or cheese, make sure that it is in a warm room between 26°C (79°F) and 32°C (90°F). Fermentation rates differ, depending on the different room conditions. You may need to allow the fermentation to continue for up to another 7 hours.

## STORING STAPLES

- It is important to sterilise jars and lids if you are going to store products such as jam, marmalade, cashew cheese and dehydrated vegetables. Simply boil the jars and lids for 10 minutes and allow them to cool and dry naturally.

# QUICK IDEAS

I use truffle salt in everything that is savoury, and vanilla salt for sweets. Saffron salt is brilliant for sweets, and savoury dishes that don't have onion or garlic or other spices. The same applies to the sprinkles, which are terrific in salads. As you'd expect, the chocolate soil makes an ideal match for the ice-creams.

The sweeteners are also great to use in many recipes. Instead of using a neutral flavour of sweeteners, add a little depth by making them flavoured, so when you use them in your desserts, they create a finer taste on your palate.

Use your cashew dairy products as you would your normal dairy products. Cashew dairy has a lovely clean flavour due to the nature of the products that have been chosen. (Personally, I love this section as I am dairy intolerant.)

You can have lots of fun with the dressings by adding and testing different flavours with vegetables, fruits, nuts and herbs. Mix your Asian dressings with Asian vegetables and herbs, or mix your dairy salad dressings with leafy greens - they work very well.

The pâté recipes are delicious, but if you feel like being creative, simply make the base and add your favourite vegetables, herbs and spices for a personalised result.

All of your staples can be used in whatever form or shape you like. They are here to give you ideas to get you started, but don't rely heavily on these recipes to satisfy your palate or curiosity. Experimenting is one of the best things about cooking. Trying new things is the natural way to create recipes. Have fun and be passionate about being in the kitchen, and you'll achieve great results all by yourself.

# DEHYDRATED BABY HEIRLOOM CARROTS

MAKES 330 G (11½ OZ)

380 g (13½ oz) baby heirloom carrots, trimmed
125 ml (4 fl oz/½ cup) extra virgin olive oil
60 ml (2 fl oz/¼ cup) coconut nectar
½ teaspoon pink lake salt
2 cardamom pods, crushed
½ teaspoon fennel seeds (optional)

Combine all the ingredients in a medium bowl.

Line a baking tray with baking paper. Spread out the coated carrots on the tray and put them in the dehydrator for 12 hours, turning them every 2 hours.

Serve immediately or store in a sterilised glass jar in the refrigerator. These will keep for up to 4 days. When you're ready to use the carrots, remove them from the jar and put them on a baking tray in the dehydrator for 10–20 minutes to warm slightly and remove the chill.

# DEHYDRATED MUSHROOMS

MAKES 280 G (10 OZ)

400 g (14 oz) Swiss brown mushrooms, or mushrooms of choice
125 ml (4 fl oz/½ cup) tamari
125 ml (4 fl oz/½ cup) extra virgin olive oil

Halve the mushrooms and combine with the tamari and olive oil in a medium bowl.

Spread out the coated mushrooms on a baking tray lined with baking paper and cover with another layer of baking paper. Weight the paper down to ensure the fan in the dehydrator doesn't dislodge the paper. Place the tray in the dehydrator for 4 hours, remove the top layer of baking paper and dehydrate for a further 4 hours to caramelise the mushrooms.

Serve immediately or store in a sterilised glass jar in the refrigerator. These will keep for up to 4 days. When you're ready to use the mushrooms, remove them from the jar and put them on a baking tray in the dehydrator for 10-20 minutes to warm slightly and remove the chill.

NOTE Robust mushrooms, such as Swiss brown, shiitake and oyster mushrooms, are best dehydrated for 8 hours to develop texture and flavour. If you prefer a softer texture, dehydrate the mushrooms for a shorter time. If you prefer your mushrooms earthier and more textural, keep them in the dehydrator for longer.

# DEHYDRATED FENNEL BULBS

MAKES 200 G (7 OZ)

3 baby fennel bulbs, about 250 g (9 oz) in total
125 ml (4 fl oz/½ cup) extra virgin olive oil
60 ml (2 fl oz/¼ cup) coconut nectar
1 teaspoon fennel seeds
½ teaspoon pink lake salt

Remove the tough outer layer of the fennel bulbs. Cut the bulbs into quarters and combine with the remaining ingredients in a medium bowl.

Put the coated fennel on a baking tray lined with baking paper and cover with another layer of baking paper. Weight the paper down to ensure the fan in the dehydrator doesn't dislodge the paper. Place the tray in the dehydrator for 12 hours. Turn the fennel bulbs every 3 hours and remove the top layer of baking paper halfway through to allow caramelisation.

Serve immediately or store in a sterilised glass jar in the refrigerator. These will keep for up to 4 days. When you're ready to use the fennel, remove them from the jar and put them on a baking tray in the dehydrator for 10-20 minutes to warm slightly and remove the chill.

# DEHYDRATED TOMATOES

MAKES 150 G (5½ OZ)

200 g (7 oz) baby vine tomatoes
2 garlic cloves
60 ml (2 fl oz/¼ cup) extra virgin olive oil
¼ teaspoon pink lake salt
½ thyme sprig, roughly chopped

Remove the stems from the tomatoes. Cut the tomatoes in half lengthways and place them cut side up on a wire rack sitting on a baking tray.

Thinly slice the garlic and scatter over the tomatoes. Drizzle with the olive oil and sprinkle with the salt and thyme.

Place the baking tray in the dehydrator for 12 hours.

Serve immediately or store in a sterilised glass jar in the refrigerator. These will keep for up to 4 days. When you're ready to use the tomatoes, remove them from the jar and put them on a baking tray in the dehydrator for 10-20 minutes to warm slightly and remove the chill.

# DEHYDRATED RED ONIONS OR BABY LEEKS

MAKES 100 G (3½ OZ)

3 red onions or trimmed baby leeks, about 350 g (12 oz) in total
60 ml (2 fl oz/¼ cup) extra virgin olive oil
60 ml (2 fl oz/¼ cup) coconut nectar
½ teaspoon pink lake salt
½ teaspoon freshly ground black pepper

Cut the red onions or leeks into quarters. Combine with the remaining ingredients in a medium bowl.

Put the onions or leeks on a baking tray lined with baking paper and cover with another layer of baking paper. Weight the paper down to ensure the fan in the dehydrator doesn't dislodge the paper. Place the tray in the dehydrator for 5 hours, remove the top layer of baking paper and dehydrate for a further 5 hours to allow caramelisation.

Serve immediately or store in a sterilised glass jar in the refrigerator. These will keep for up to 4 days. When you're ready to use the onions or leeks, remove them from the jar and put them on a baking tray in the dehydrator for 10-20 minutes to warm slightly and remove the chill.

# DEHYDRATED OLIVES

MAKES 520 G (1 LB 2½ OZ)

1.1 kg (2 lb 7 oz/8 cups) olives in brine

Rinse the olives under cold running water for 1 minute and allow them to dry completely.

Put the olives on a baking tray lined with baking paper and cover with another layer of baking paper. Weight the paper down to ensure the fan in the dehydrator doesn't dislodge the paper. Place the tray in the dehydrator for 2½ hours, remove the top layer of baking paper and dehydrate for a further 2½ hours.

Serve immediately or store in a sterilised glass jar in the refrigerator. These will keep for up to 4 days. When you're ready to use the olives, remove them from the jar and put them on a baking tray in the dehydrator for 10-20 minutes to warm slightly and remove the chill.

# DEHYDRATED EGGPLANTS

MAKES 300 G (10½ OZ)

6 long thin baby eggplants (aubergines), about 500 g (1 lb 2 oz) in total
250 ml (9 fl oz/1 cup) extra virgin olive oil
60 ml (2 fl oz/¼ cup) coconut nectar
1 tablespoon tamari
1 tablespoon miso paste
1 teaspoon coriander seeds
½ teaspoon pink lake salt
½ teaspoon freshly ground black pepper

Cut the eggplants in half lengthways. Combine with the remaining ingredients in a medium bowl.

Put the eggplants on a baking tray lined with baking paper and cover with another layer of baking paper. Weight the paper down to ensure the fan in the dehydrator doesn't dislodge the paper. Place the tray in the dehydrator for 9 hours, remove the top layer of baking paper and dehydrate for a further 9 hours to allow caramelisation.

Serve immediately or store in a sterilised glass jar in the refrigerator. These will keep for up to 4 days. When you're ready to use the eggplants, remove them from the jar and put them on a baking tray in the dehydrator for 10–20 minutes to warm slightly and remove the chill.

TIP If you want to take the eggplant skins off, pour hot water into a large bowl, place all the eggplants in the bowl and cover with plastic wrap. Leave for 5 minutes. Run the eggplants under cold water and peel off the skin gently with a palette knife.

# DEHYDRATED CAPSICUMS

MAKES 250 G (9 OZ)

250 g (9 oz) red capsicums (peppers)
250 g (9 oz) green capsicums (peppers)
500 ml (17 fl oz/2 cups) extra virgin olive oil
6 garlic cloves
1 tablespoon lemon juice
1 tablespoon tamari
1 tablespoon coconut nectar
1 tablespoon apple cider vinegar
3 mint sprigs, leaves picked
3 flat-leaf (Italian) parsley sprigs, leaves picked
½ teaspoon pink lake salt
½ teaspoon freshly ground black pepper

Cut the capsicums into quarters and remove the seeds and membranes. Combine with the remaining ingredients in a large bowl.

Put the capsicum quarters on a baking tray lined with baking paper and cover with another layer of baking paper. Weight the paper down to ensure the fan in the dehydrator doesn't dislodge the paper. Place the tray in the dehydrator for 9 hours. Remove the top layer of baking paper, turn the capsicums and dehydrate for a further 9 hours to allow caramelisation.

Serve immediately. Alternatively, store the capsicums in a sterilised glass jar in the refrigerator. These will keep for up to 4 days. When you're ready to use the capsicums, remove them from the jar and put them on a baking tray in the dehydrator for 10-20 minutes to warm slightly and remove the chill.

# DEHYDRATED BABY ZUCCHINI

MAKES 150 G (5½ OZ)

12 baby zucchini (courgettes), about 200 g (7 oz) in total
125 ml (4 fl oz/½ cup) extra virgin olive oil
6 garlic cloves
1 tablespoon lemon juice
2 tablespoons tamari
2 tablespoons coconut nectar
1 teaspoon pink lake salt
1 teaspoon freshly ground black pepper

Cut the zucchini in half lengthways and combine them with the remaining ingredients in a medium bowl.

Put the zucchini on a baking tray lined with baking paper and cover with another layer of baking paper. Weight the paper down to ensure the fan in the dehydrator doesn't dislodge the paper. Place the tray in the dehydrator for 8 hours, turning them every 2 hours. Remove the top layer of baking paper halfway through to allow caramelisation.

Serve immediately or store in a sterilised glass jar in the refrigerator. These will keep for up to 4 days. When you're ready to use the zucchini, remove them from the jar and put them on a baking tray in the dehydrator for 10–20 minutes to warm slightly and remove the chill.

# DEHYDRATED GARLIC

MAKES 385 G (13½ OZ)

6 garlic bulbs, about 400 g (14 oz) in total
185 ml (6 fl oz/¾ cup) extra virgin olive oil
1 tablespoon coconut nectar
1 teaspoon pink lake salt
½ teaspoon freshly ground black pepper

Cut the garlic bulbs in half crossways. Combine the garlic with the remaining ingredients in a medium bowl.

Put the garlic cut side down on a baking tray lined with baking paper and cover with another layer of baking paper. Weight the paper down to ensure the fan in the dehydrator doesn't dislodge the paper. Place the tray in the dehydrator for 10 hours. Remove the top layer of baking paper, turn the garlic and dehydrate for a further 10 hours to allow caramelisation.

Serve immediately or store in a sterilised glass jar in a cool, dry place. These will keep for up to approximately 2 weeks.

# DEHYDRATED BABY BEETROOT

MAKES 150 G (5½ OZ)

6 baby beetroot (beets), about 225 g (8 oz) in total
125 ml (4 fl oz/½ cup) extra virgin olive oil
6 garlic cloves
1 tablespoon lemon juice
2 tablespoons tamari
2 tablespoons coconut nectar
2 tablespoons apple cider vinegar
½ teaspoon pink lake salt
½ teaspoon freshly ground black pepper

Peel or wash the beetroot well. Combine with the remaining ingredients in a medium bowl.

Put the beetroot on a baking tray lined with baking paper and cover with another layer of baking paper. Weight the paper down to ensure the fan in the dehydrator doesn't dislodge the paper. Place the tray in the dehydrator for 9 hours, remove the top layer of baking paper and dehydrate for a further 9 hours to caramelise the beetroot.

Serve immediately or store in a sterilised glass jar in the refrigerator. These will keep for up to 4 days. When you're ready to use the beetroot, remove them from the jar and put them on a baking tray in the dehydrator for 10-20 minutes to warm slightly and remove the chill.

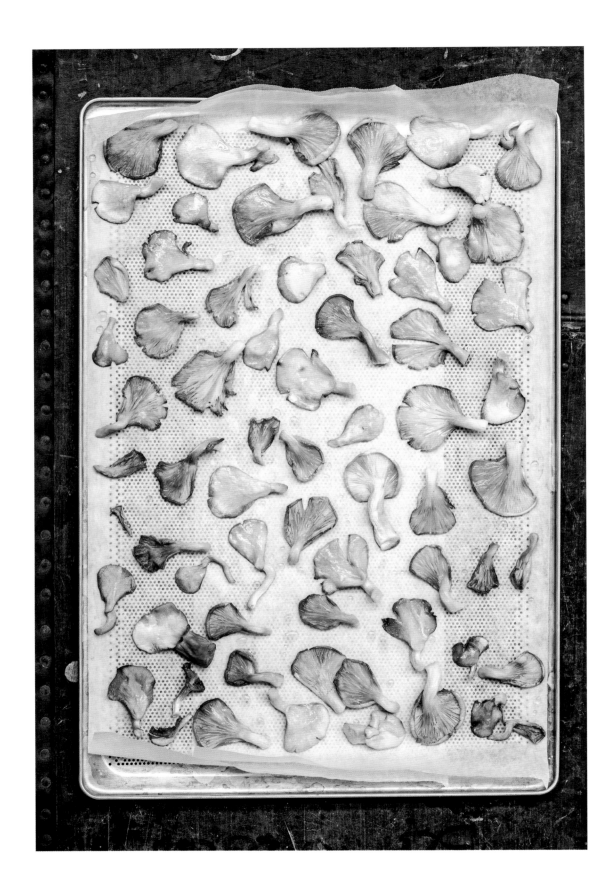

# CASHEW MILK

MAKES 700 ML (24 FL OZ)

155 g (5½ oz/1 cup) cashews
625 ml (21½ fl oz/2½ cups) water
½ teaspoon vanilla bean paste (page 118)
¼ teaspoon pink lake salt

Put all the ingredients in a blender and blend until smooth.

Refrigerate for 2 hours to chill or consume as is.

NOTE The consistency of this cashew milk is similar to full-fat milk. It's perfect to use on mueslis and other cereals, and to make smoothies and other milk drinks. If you prefer a different consistency, add less or more water as desired.

# VANILLA CASHEW CREAM

MAKES 420 G (14¾ OZ)

155 g (5½ oz/1 cup) cashews
125 ml (4 fl oz/½ cup) water
60 ml (2 fl oz/¼ cup) coconut nectar
2 tablespoons rum
2 teaspoons vanilla bean paste (page 118)
¼ teaspoon vanilla salt (page 103)
125 ml (4 fl oz/½ cup) coconut oil

Put the cashews and water in a blender and mix for about 30 seconds (depending on your blender) until you have a smooth paste. Blend slowly at first, then increase to high. This will ensure you achieve a lovely light consistency.

Add the coconut nectar, rum, vanilla bean paste and vanilla salt, and blend for 10 seconds.

Add the coconut oil and blend for another 5 seconds, or until just combined. Refrigerate for 12 hours to set.

# CASHEW YOGHURT

MAKES 1 KG (2 LB 4 OZ)

BASE
375 g (13 oz) cashews
310 ml (10¾ fl oz/1¼ cups) water
1 probiotic capsule

FLAVOUR
310 ml (10¾ fl oz/1¼ cups) water
80 ml (2½ fl oz/⅓ cup) extra virgin olive oil
60 ml (2 fl oz/¼ cup) coconut nectar
30 g (1 oz/1 tablespoon) vanilla bean paste (page 118)
1 teaspoon sunflower lecithin
1 teaspoon carob bean gum

To make the base, put the cashews and water in a blender and mix for about 30 seconds (depending on your blender) until you have a smooth paste. Blend slowly at first, then increase to high. This will ensure you achieve a lovely light consistency for your base.

Break the probiotic capsule in half and add the contents to the cashew mix. Blend on low for 20 seconds, taking care not to overheat.

Pour into a glass bowl, cover with baking paper, and use masking tape to seal the top. Set the bowl aside in a warm place (ideally 26–32°C/79–90°F) for 15 hours to culture. The fermented cashew mix should have a dough-like consistency with small air pockets, and should smell sweet with a hint of sourness. If the mix is still runny and smells simply sweet, it's not ready. Ferment for up to another 7 hours if necessary. Check every few hours to ensure you achieve the right consistency.

Transfer the cashew mix to a food processor, add the flavour ingredients and process for 10 seconds.

Refrigerate for 24 hours before consuming.

NOTE ON FERMENTATION Due to differing humidity levels, the fermentation process can vary and therefore the amount of moisture in the cashew mix can vary, affecting the final weight of the base product. Fermentation times will differ from place to place, depending on the level of humidity in the air.

# CLASSIC FROZEN CASHEW YOGHURT

MAKES 660 G (1 LB 7 OZ)

BASE
155 g (5½ oz/1 cup) cashews
250 ml (9 fl oz/1 cup) water
1 probiotic capsule

FLAVOUR
250 ml (9 fl oz/1 cup) water
125 ml (4 fl oz/½ cup) coconut nectar
2 tablespoons rum
2 teaspoons vanilla bean paste (page 118)
¼ teaspoon vanilla salt (page 103)
1 teaspoon sunflower lecithin
1 teaspoon guar gum
1 teaspoon carob bean gum
1 cardamom pod, seeds only

To make the base, put the cashews and water in a blender and mix for about 30 seconds (depending on your blender) until you have a smooth paste. Blend slowly at first, then increase to high. This will ensure you achieve a lovely light consistency for your base.

Break the probiotic capsule in half and add the contents to the cashew mix. Blend on low for 20 seconds, taking care not to overheat.

Pour into a glass bowl, cover with baking paper, and use masking tape to seal the top. Set the bowl aside in a warm place (ideally 26-32°C/79-90°F) for 15 hours to culture. The fermented cashew mix should have a dough-like consistency with small air pockets, and should smell sweet with a hint of sourness. If the mix is still runny and smells simply sweet, it's not ready. Ferment for up to another 7 hours if necessary. Check every few hours to ensure you achieve the right consistency.

Put the base and the remaining quantity of water in a blender and mix for 2 minutes. Add the remaining flavour ingredients, and blend for a further 2 minutes.

Churn in an ice-cream machine according to the manufacturer's instructions, or pour into a container, cover and freeze for about 12 hours or until frozen.

# CASHEW MAYONNAISE

MAKES 800 G (1 LB 12 OZ)

BASE
340 g (12 oz/2¼ cups) cashews
250 ml (9 fl oz/1 cup) water
1 probiotic capsule

FLAVOUR
250 ml (9 fl oz/1 cup) extra virgin olive oil
125 ml (4 fl oz/½ cup) water
60 ml (2 fl oz/¼ cup) lemon juice
1 tablespoon apple cider vinegar
½ teaspoon pink lake salt
½ teaspoon freshly ground black pepper
½ teaspoon yellow mustard seeds, ground

To make the base, put the cashews and water in a blender and mix for about 30 seconds (depending on your blender) until you have a smooth paste. Blend slowly at first, then increase to high. This will ensure you achieve a lovely light consistency for your base.

Break the probiotic capsule in half and add the contents to the cashew mix. Blend on low for 20 seconds, taking care not to overheat.

Pour into a glass bowl, cover with baking paper, and use masking tape to seal the top. Set the bowl aside in a warm place (ideally 26–32°C/79–90°F) for 15 hours to culture. The fermented cashew mix should have a dough-like consistency with small air pockets, and should smell sweet with a hint of sourness. If the mix is still runny and smells simply sweet, it's not ready. Ferment for up to another 7 hours if necessary. Check the consistency every few hours.

Transfer the mix to a food processor, add the flavour ingredients and process for 10 seconds.

Refrigerate for 24 hours before consuming.

NOTE ON FERMENTATION Due to differing humidity levels, the fermentation process can vary and therefore the amount of moisture in the cashew mix can vary, affecting the final weight of the base product. Fermentation times will differ from place to place, depending on the level of humidity in the air.

# CLASSIC CASHEW CHEESE

MAKES 600 G (1 LB 5 OZ)

BASE
195 g (7 oz/1 ¼ cups) cashews
250 ml (9 fl oz/1 cup) water
1 probiotic capsule

FLAVOUR
125 ml (4 fl oz/½ cup) extra virgin olive oil
80 ml (2½ fl oz/⅓ cup) lemon juice
1 garlic clove, grated
1 French shallot, grated
½ teaspoon pink lake salt
½ teaspoon freshly ground black pepper

To make the base, put the cashews and water in a blender and mix for about 30 seconds (depending on your blender) until you have a smooth paste. Blend slowly at first, then increase to high. This will ensure you achieve a lovely light consistency for your base.

Break the probiotic capsule in half and add the contents to the cashew mix. Blend on low for 20 seconds, taking care not to overheat.

Pour into a glass bowl, cover with baking paper, and use masking tape to seal the top. Set the bowl aside in a warm place (ideally 26-32°C/79-90°F) for 15 hours to culture. The fermented cashew mix should have a dough-like consistency with small air pockets, and should smell sweet with a hint of sourness. If the mix is still runny and smells simply sweet, it's not ready. Ferment for up to another 7 hours if necessary. Check every few hours to ensure you achieve the right consistency.

Transfer the cashew mix to a food processor, add the flavour ingredients and process for 10 seconds.

Refrigerate for 24 hours before consuming.

NOTE ON FERMENTATION Due to differing humidity levels, the fermentation process can vary and therefore the amount of moisture in the cashew mix can vary, affecting the final weight of the base product. Fermentation times will differ from place to place, depending on the level of humidity in the air.

# LEMON AND DILL CASHEW CHEESE

MAKES 625 G (1 LB 6 OZ)

BASE
195 g (7 oz/1¼ cups) cashews
250 ml (9 fl oz/1 cup) water
1 probiotic capsule

FLAVOUR
1 handful dill leaves, about 10 g (¼ oz)
125 ml (4 fl oz/½ cup) extra virgin olive oil
80 ml (2½ fl oz/⅓ cup) lemon juice
1 garlic clove, grated
1 French shallot, grated
½ teaspoon pink lake salt
½ teaspoon freshly ground black pepper

To make the base, put the cashews and water in a blender and mix for about 30 seconds (depending on your blender) until you have a smooth paste. Blend slowly at first, then increase to high. This will ensure you achieve a lovely light consistency for your base.

Break the probiotic capsule in half and add the contents to the cashew mix. Blend on low for 20 seconds, taking care not to overheat.

Pour into a glass bowl, cover with baking paper, and use masking tape to seal the top. Set the bowl aside in a warm place (ideally 26-32°C/79-90°F) for 15 hours to culture. The fermented cashew mix should have a dough-like consistency with small air pockets, and should smell sweet with a hint of sourness. If the mix is still runny and smells simply sweet, it's not ready. Ferment for up to another 7 hours if necessary. Check every few hours to ensure you achieve the right consistency.

Transfer the cashew mix to a food processor, add the flavour ingredients and process for 10 seconds.

Refrigerate for 24 hours before consuming.

# WALNUT CASHEW CHEESE

MAKES 625 G (1 LB 6 OZ)

BASE
195 g (7 oz/1¼ cups) cashews
250 ml (9 fl oz/1 cup) water
1 probiotic capsule

FLAVOUR
125 ml (4 fl oz/½ cup) extra virgin olive oil
2 tablespoons lemon juice
½ teaspoon pink lake salt
½ teaspoon freshly ground black pepper
70 g (2½ oz/½ cup) walnut pieces

To make the base, place the cashews and water in a blender and mix for about 30 seconds (depending on your blender) until you have a smooth paste. Blend slowly at first, then increase to high. This will ensure you achieve a lovely light consistency for your base.

Break the probiotic capsule in half and add the contents to the cashew mix. Blend on low for 20 seconds, taking care not to overheat.

Pour into a glass bowl, cover with baking paper, and use masking tape to seal the top. Set the bowl aside in a warm place (ideally 26-32°C/79-90°F) for 15 hours to culture. The fermented cashew mix should have a dough-like consistency with small air pockets, and should smell sweet with a hint of sourness. If the mix is still runny and smells simply sweet, it's not ready. Ferment for up to another 7 hours if necessary. Check every few hours to ensure you achieve the right consistency.

Transfer to a food processor, add the olive oil, lemon juice, pink lake salt and pepper, and process for 10 seconds. Add the walnuts and process for a further 10 seconds.

Refrigerate for 24 hours before consuming.

NOTE ON FERMENTATION Due to differing humidity levels, the fermentation process can vary and therefore the amount of moisture in the cashew mix can vary, affecting the final weight of the base product. Fermentation times will differ from place to place, depending on the level of humidity in the air.

# GARLIC AND CHIVE CASHEW CHEESE

MAKES 625 G (1 LB 6 OZ)

BASE
195 g (7 oz/1¼ cups) cashews
250 ml (9 fl oz/1 cup) water
1 probiotic capsule

FLAVOUR
125 ml (4 fl oz/½ cup) extra virgin olive oil
30 g (1 oz/½ cup) finely chopped chives
80 ml (2½ fl oz/⅓ cup) lemon juice
3 garlic cloves, grated
1 French shallot, grated
½ teaspoon pink lake salt
½ teaspoon freshly ground black pepper

To make the base, put the cashews and water in a blender and mix for about 30 seconds (depending on your blender) until you have a smooth paste. Blend slowly at first, then increase to high. This will ensure you achieve a lovely light consistency for your base.

Break the probiotic capsule in half and add the contents to the cashew mix. Blend on low for 20 seconds, taking care not to overheat.

Pour into a glass bowl, cover with baking paper, and use masking tape to seal the top. Set the bowl aside in a warm place (ideally 26-32°C/79-90°F) for 15 hours to culture. The fermented cashew mix should have a dough-like consistency with small air pockets, and should smell sweet with a hint of sourness. If the mix is still runny and smells simply sweet, it's not ready. Ferment for up to another 7 hours if necessary. Check every few hours to ensure you achieve the right consistency.

Transfer to a food processor with the remaining ingredients and process for 10 seconds.

Refrigerate for 24 hours before consuming.

# CASHEW MASCARPONE

MAKES 750 G (1 LB 10 OZ)

235 g (8½ oz/1½ cups) cashews
250 ml (9 fl oz/1 cup) water
125 ml (4 fl oz/½ cup) coconut nectar
70 ml (2¼ fl oz) lemon juice
2½ tablespoons rum
1 teaspoon vanilla bean paste (page 118)
¼ teaspoon vanilla salt (page 103)
250 ml (9 fl oz/1 cup) coconut oil, melted

Put the cashews and water in a blender and mix for about 30 seconds (depending on your blender) until you have a smooth paste. Blend slowly at first, then increase to high. This will create a lovely foundation, and will ensure you achieve a good consistency for the mascarpone.

Add the coconut nectar, lemon juice, rum, vanilla bean paste and vanilla salt, and blend for 10 seconds.

Add the coconut oil and blend at a low speed for a further 5 seconds until just combined. To achieve a lovely light consistency, avoid blending the fats at high speed.

Refrigerate for 4 hours to set.

# FRENCH VANILLA ICE-CREAM

MAKES 600 G (1 LB 5 OZ)

155 g (5½ oz/1 cup) cashews
250 ml (9 fl oz/1 cup) water
125 ml (4 fl oz/½ cup) coconut nectar
2 tablespoons rum
2 teaspoons vanilla bean paste (page 118)
¼ teaspoon vanilla salt (page 103)
1 teaspoon sunflower lecithin
1 teaspoon guar gum
1 teaspoon carob bean gum
1 cardamom pod, seeds only

Put the cashews and water in a blender and mix for about 30 seconds (depending on your blender) until you have a smooth paste. Blend slowly at first, then increase to high. This will ensure you achieve a lovely light consistency.

Add the remaining ingredients, and blend for a further 2 minutes.

Churn in an ice-cream machine according to the manufacturer's instructions, or pour into a container, cover and freeze for about 12 hours or until frozen.

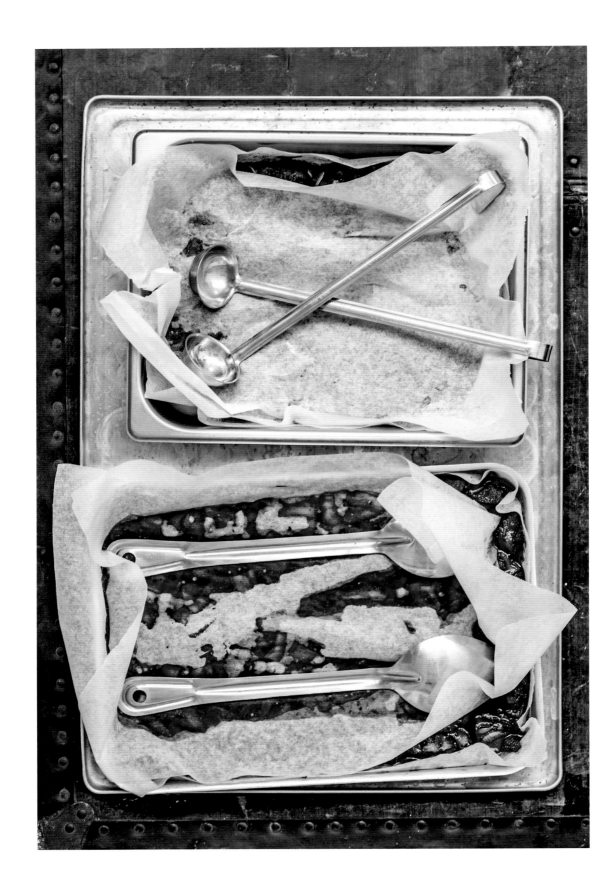

STRAWBERRY AND PEPPERBERRY JAM

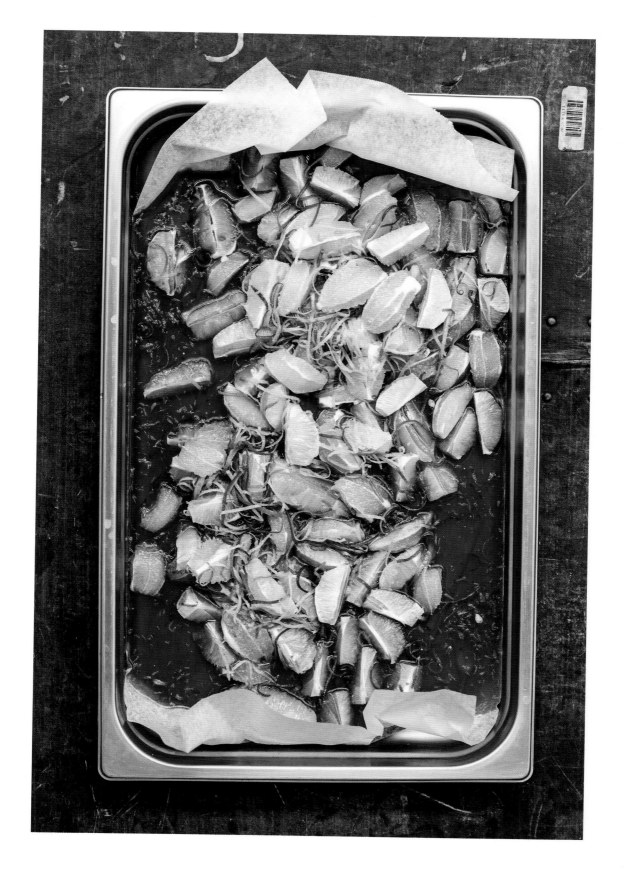

LEMON AND LIME MARMALADE

# STRAWBERRY AND PEPPERBERRY JAM

MAKES 640 G (1 LB 7 OZ)

1 kg (2 lb 4 oz) strawberries, hulled and sliced
500 ml (17 fl oz/2 cups) coconut nectar
60 ml (2 fl oz/¼ cup) lemon juice
1 tablespoon vanilla bean paste (page 118)
1 teaspoon vanilla salt (page 103)
2 teaspoons guar gum
1 tablespoon pepperberries
2 cardamom pods, seeds only

Gently combine the strawberries, coconut nectar, lemon juice, vanilla bean paste, vanilla salt and guar gum in a large bowl. Place the pepperberries and cardamom in a piece of muslin (cheesecloth), tie with string to enclose, and add to the bowl.

Spread the mixture (including the muslin bag) on a baking tray lined with baking paper and cover with another layer of baking paper. Weight the paper down to ensure the fan in the dehydrator doesn't dislodge the paper. Put the tray in the dehydrator for approximately 8 hours.

Remove the tray from the dehydrator, remove the top layer of baking paper, stir the mixture and then return to the dehydrator for a further 7 hours, uncovered, to ensure a lovely caramelised finish.

Spoon the jam into one large sterilised glass jar with the muslin and refrigerate. This will keep for up to 1 month.

# VANILLA PEACH JAM

MAKES 1 KG (2 LB 4 OZ)

1.3 kg (3 lb) peaches, sliced and stones discarded
625 ml (21½ fl oz/2½ cups) coconut nectar
60 ml (2 fl oz/¼ cup) lemon juice
1½ tablespoons rum
4 tablespoons vanilla bean paste (page 118)
½ teaspoon vanilla salt (page 103)
2 teaspoons guar gum

Spread the peach pieces straight on the mesh in the dehydrator. Combine all the other ingredients in a baking tray and slot that in on another level in the dehydrator. Dehydrate both for 8 hours.

Combine the liquid and peaches in a baking tray lined with baking paper and cover with another layer of baking paper. Weight the paper down to ensure the fan in the dehydrator doesn't dislodge the paper. Dehydrate for 4 hours.

Remove the tray from the dehydrator, remove the top layer of baking paper, stir the mixture and then return to the dehydrator for a further 4 hours, uncovered, to ensure a lovely caramelised finish.

Spoon the jam into sterilised glass jars and refrigerate. This will keep for up to 2 weeks.

# PEAR AND MUSCATEL JAM

MAKES 800 G (1 LB 12 OZ)

1 kg (2 lb 4 oz) beurre bosc pears, or pears of choice
3 small oranges, peeled and sliced
85 g (3 oz/½ cup) muscatel raisins or raisins
750 ml (26 fl oz/3 cups) coconut nectar
125 ml (4 fl oz/½ cup) port
1 tablespoon vanilla salt (page 103)
2 teaspoons vanilla bean paste (page 118)
½ teaspoon ground cinnamon
2 cardamom pods, seeds only
2 teaspoons guar gum

Cut the pears into quarters, removing the cores. Spread the pear quarters on a baking tray lined with baking paper. Combine all the other ingredients and pour into a baking tray lined with baking paper. Place both trays in the dehydrator for 15 hours.

Combine the pears and liquid in a baking tray lined with baking paper and cover with another layer of baking paper. Weight the paper down to ensure the fan in the dehydrator doesn't dislodge the paper. Dehydrate for 4 hours.

Remove the tray from the dehydrator, remove the top layer of baking paper, stir the mixture and then return to the dehydrator for a further 4 hours, uncovered, to ensure a lovely caramelised finish.

Put the mixture in a food processor and pulse for 10 seconds.

Spoon the jam into sterilised glass jars and refrigerate. This will keep for up to 3 months.

# FIG JAM

MAKES 800 G (1 LB 12 OZ)

1.3 kg (3 lb) fresh figs, cut into quarters
750 ml (26 fl oz/3 cups) coconut nectar
125 ml (4 fl oz/½ cup) balsamic vinegar
125 ml (4 fl oz/½ cup) rum
2 teaspoons ground cinnamon
1 tablespoon vanilla bean paste (page 118)
1½ teaspoons vanilla salt (page 103)
2 teaspoons guar gum

Spread the fig pieces straight on the mesh in the dehydrator. Combine all the other ingredients in a baking tray and slot that in on another level in the dehydrator. Dehydrate both for 8 hours.

Combine the liquid and figs in a baking tray lined with baking paper and cover with another layer of baking paper. Weight the paper down to ensure the fan in the dehydrator doesn't dislodge the paper. Dehydrate for 4 hours.

Remove the tray from the dehydrator, remove the top layer of baking paper, stir the mixture and then return to the dehydrator for a further 4 hours, uncovered, to ensure a lovely caramelised finish.

Spoon the jam into sterilised glass jars and refrigerate. This will keep for up to 3 months.

# CUMQUAT AND BRANDY MARMALADE

MAKES 800 G (1 LB 12 OZ)

500 g (1 lb 2 oz) cumquats, halved
500 ml (17 fl oz/2 cups) coconut nectar
250 ml (9 fl oz/1 cup) brandy
1 teaspoon vanilla salt (page 103)

Combine all the ingredients in a large bowl.

Spread the mixture on a baking tray lined with baking paper and cover with another layer of baking paper. Weight the paper down to ensure the fan in the dehydrator doesn't dislodge the paper. Dehydrate for 10 hours.

Remove the tray from the dehydrator, remove the top layer of baking paper, stir the mixture and then return to the dehydrator for a further 10 hours, uncovered, to ensure a lovely caramelised finish.

Spoon the marmalade into sterilised glass jars and refrigerate. This will keep for up to 3 months.

# SAFFRON ORANGE MARMALADE

MAKES 1 KG (2 LB 4 OZ)

2 kg (4 lb 8 oz) oranges
1 litre (35 fl oz/4 cups) coconut nectar
1 g saffron threads
2 teaspoons guar gum

Zest the oranges with a zester and reserve the zest. Peel off the white pith and cut the oranges into quarters and then into quarters again.

Combine the orange pieces, orange zest and remaining ingredients in a large bowl.

Spread the mixture on a baking tray lined with baking paper and cover with another layer of baking paper. Weight the paper down to ensure the fan in the dehydrator doesn't dislodge the paper. Dehydrate for 13 hours.

Remove the tray from the dehydrator, remove the top layer of baking paper, stir the mixture and then return to the dehydrator for a further 12 hours, uncovered, to ensure a lovely caramelised finish.

Spoon the marmalade into sterilised glass jars and refrigerate. This will keep for up to 3 months.

# LEMON AND LIME MARMALADE

MAKES 750 G (1 LB 10 OZ)

1 kg (2 lb 4 oz) lemons
500 g (1 lb 2 oz) limes
750 ml (26 fl oz/3 cups) coconut nectar

Zest the lemons and limes with a zester, and reserve the zest. Peel off the white pith and cut the fruit into quarters and then into quarters again.

Combine the citrus pieces and zest with the coconut nectar in a large bowl.

Spread the mixture on a baking tray lined with baking paper and cover with another layer of baking paper. Weight the paper down to ensure the fan in the dehydrator doesn't dislodge the paper. Dehydrate for 13 hours.

Remove the tray from the dehydrator, remove the top layer of baking paper, stir the mixture and then return to the dehydrator for a further 12 hours, uncovered, to ensure a lovely caramelised finish.

Spoon the marmalade into sterilised glass jars and refrigerate. This will keep for up to 3 months.

# BLACK FOREST COMPOTE

MAKES 750 G (1 LB 10 OZ)

270 g (9½ oz/1¾ cups) blueberries
310 g (11 oz/2½ cups) raspberries
zest of 6 oranges
1 litre (35 fl oz/4 cups) coconut nectar
250 ml (9 fl oz/1 cup) port
1 tablespoon vanilla salt (page 103)
1 tablespoon vanilla bean paste (page 118)

Combine all the ingredients in a large bowl.

Spread the mixture on a baking tray lined with baking paper and cover with another layer of baking paper. Weight the paper down to ensure the fan in the dehydrator doesn't dislodge the paper. Dehydrate for 3 hours.

Remove the tray from the dehydrator, remove the top layer of baking paper, stir the mixture and then return to the dehydrator for a further 3 hours, uncovered, to ensure a lovely caramelised finish.

Spoon the mixture into sterilised glass jars and refrigerate. This will keep for up to 3 months.

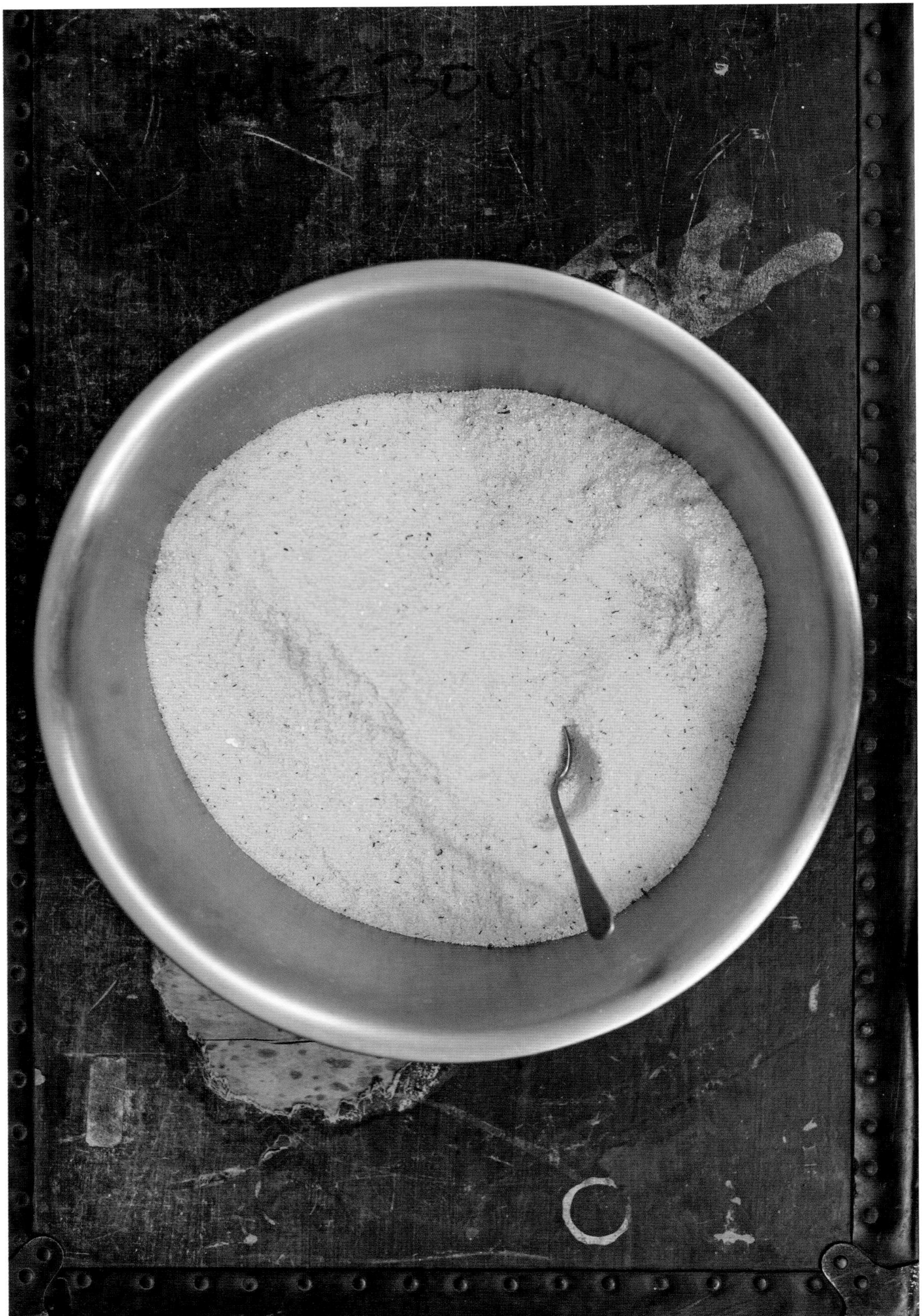

# TRUFFLE SALT

MAKES 500 G (1 LB 2 OZ/2 CUPS)

2 g fresh local truffles
500 g (1 lb 2 oz/2 cups) pink lake salt

Put the truffle and salt in a food processor and process for 10 seconds.

Pour the salt onto a baking tray lined with baking paper and place in the dehydrator for 2 hours.

Remove the tray from the dehydrator and set aside, uncovered, for 6 hours to air-dry.

Store in sterilised glass jars in a cool dry place.

# SAFFRON SALT

MAKES 500 G (1 LB 2 OZ/2 CUPS)

1 teaspoon saffron threads
500 g (1 lb 2 oz/2 cups) pink lake salt
80 ml (2½ fl oz/⅓ cup) rosewater

Put the saffron, salt and rosewater in a food processor and process for 10 seconds.

Pour the salt onto a baking tray lined with baking paper and place in the dehydrator for 4 hours.

Remove the tray from the dehydrator and set aside, uncovered, for 6 hours to air-dry.

Store in sterilised glass jars in a cool dry place.

# LEMON SALT

MAKES 500 G (1 LB 2 OZ/2 CUPS)

1 lemon, roughly chopped
500 g (1 lb 2 oz/2 cups) pink lake salt

Put the lemon and salt in a food processor and process for 20 seconds.

Pour the salt onto a baking tray lined with baking paper and place in the dehydrator for 8 hours.

Remove the tray from the dehydrator and set aside, uncovered, for 6 hours to air-dry.

Store in sterilised glass jars in a cool dry place.

# VANILLA SALT

MAKES 550 G (1 LB 4 OZ)

500 g (1 lb 2 oz/2 cups) pink lake salt
80 g (2¾ oz) vanilla bean paste (page 118)

Put the salt and vanilla bean paste in a food processor and process for 10 seconds.

Pour onto a baking tray lined with baking paper and place in the dehydrator for 2 hours.

Remove the tray from the dehydrator and set aside, uncovered, for 6 hours to air-dry.

Store in sterilised glass jars in a cool dry place.

NOTE ABOUT SALTS Different salt varieties have different weight measures due to their differing mineral content. If using a different salt, follow the weight in grams or ounces rather than the cup measurement.

# FURAKAKI SPRINKLE

MAKES 440 G (15½ OZ)

30 g (1 oz) fresh ginger, sliced
290 g (10¼ oz/2 cups) white sesame seeds
145 g (5 oz/1 cup) black sesame seeds
17 g (½ oz/¼ cup) dulse flakes
2 tablespoons pink lake salt

Spread the ginger on a baking tray lined with baking paper and place in the dehydrator for 8 hours.

Place the ginger in a food processor with the other ingredients and process for 10 seconds.

Store in sterilised glass jars in a cool dry place.

# AEGEAN SPRINKLE

MAKES 160 G (5¾ OZ)

6 lemons
8 large tomatoes, chopped
150 g (5½ oz/1 cup) pitted olives

Zest the lemons with a zester and set zest aside. Peel off the white pith and chop the lemon flesh. Cut the tomatoes into quarters.

Spread the tomatoes, olives and chopped lemon flesh on a baking tray lined with baking paper. Place the tray into the dehydrator and dehydrate for 30 hours.

Sprinkle the tomatoes, olives and lemon flesh with the lemon zest and dehydrate for a further 2 hours.

Put the dehydrated ingredients in a blender and blend on high for 1 minute.

Store in sterilised glass jars in a cool dry place.

# SWEET TART BASES

MAKES 4 TARTS

310 g (11 oz/2 cups) cashews
2 tablespoons water
1 tablespoon coconut nectar
1 tablespoon mesquite powder or lucuma powder
½ teaspoon vanilla salt (page 103)

Put the cashews in a food processor and process for 10 seconds until the cashews are finely ground but with a bit of texture. Put the ground cashews in a medium bowl with the water and knead until it forms a dough. Add the remaining ingredients and knead to combine.

Place four 8 cm (3¼ in) diameter pastry rings on a baking tray lined with baking paper and divide the mixture evenly between the rings, pressing to cover the base. Place the baking tray in the dehydrator for 4 hours. Remove the tray from the dehydrator and remove the rings from the tarts. Return the tray of tarts to the dehydrator for a further 2 hours.

# SAVOURY TART BASES

MAKES 4 TARTS

310 g (11 oz/2 cups) cashews
2 tablespoons water
1 garlic clove
1 tablespoon extra virgin olive oil
½ teaspoon pink lake salt

Put the cashews in a food processor and process for 10 seconds until the cashews are finely ground but with a bit of texture. Put the ground cashews in a medium bowl with the water and knead until it forms a dough. Finely grate the garlic and add to the dough with the olive oil and salt. Knead to combine.

Place four 8 cm (3¼ in) diameter rings on a baking tray lined with baking paper and divide the mixture evenly between the rings, pressing to cover the bases. Place the baking tray in the dehydrator for 4 hours. Remove the tray from the dehydrator and remove the rings from the tarts. Return the tray of tarts to the dehydrator for a further 2 hours.

# BISCUITS

MAKES 550 G (1 LB 4 OZ)

310 g (11 oz/2 cups) cashews
250 ml (9 fl oz/1 cup) water
2 tablespoons coconut nectar
1 tablespoon rum
1 tablespoon freshly brewed coffee
1 teaspoon mesquite powder or lucuma powder
½ teaspoon vanilla salt (page 103)

Put all the ingredients in a food processor and process for 3 minutes.

Line a baking tray with baking paper and spread the mixture on the tray, making sure it is thinly spread. You may need to use more than one tray. Place the baking tray(s) in the dehydrator for 36 hours.

Cut the biscuits into small pieces, scatter on a baking tray lined with baking paper and cover with a cloth. Store in the refrigerator. These will keep for up to 5 days.

# CHOCOLATE SOIL

MAKES 240 G (8½ OZ)

zest of 2 oranges
100 g (3½ oz/1 cup) cacao powder
2 tablespoons vanilla bean paste (page 118)
2 tablespoons coconut oil, melted
2 tablespoons cacao butter, melted
½ teaspoon vanilla salt (page 103)

Put all the ingredients in a medium bowl and mix well by hand (wear food-safe gloves if necessary).

Spread the mixture onto a baking tray lined with baking paper and place the tray into the dehydrator for 5 hours.

Put the mixture in a food processor and process for 10 seconds.

Pour onto a baking tray lined with baking paper and set aside, uncovered, for 1 hour to air-dry.

Store in sterilised glass jars in a cool dry place. This will keep for up to 2 weeks.


# CHOCOLATE AND COFFEE AGAVE SYRUP

MAKES 1 LITRE (35 FL OZ/4 CUPS)

1 litre (35 fl oz/4 cups) light agave syrup
60 ml (2 fl oz/¼ cup) freshly brewed coffee
½ tablespoon chocolate oil

Put all the ingredients in a large sterilised glass jar and gently shake to combine. This will keep for up to 3 months in a cool dry place.

# CINNAMON ORANGE AGAVE SYRUP

MAKES 1 LITRE (35 FL OZ/4 CUPS)

1 litre (35 fl oz/4 cups) light agave syrup
1 teaspoon orange oil
1 tablespoon ground cinnamon
½ star anise

Put all the ingredients in a large sterilised glass jar and gently shake to combine. This will keep for up to 3 months in a cool dry place.

# BLUEBERRY PORT AGAVE SYRUP

MAKES 1 LITRE (35 FL OZ/4 CUPS)

310 g (11 oz/2 cups) blueberries
500 ml (17 fl oz/2 cups) port
375 ml (13 fl oz/1½ cups) light agave syrup

Put the blueberries on a baking tray lined with baking paper and place the tray in the dehydrator for 4 hours.

Put the dehydrated blueberries in a bowl, pour over the port and soak for 4 hours.

Remove the blueberries from the port by pouring through a sieve, reserving the port liquid (the blueberries are not used).

Pour the port liquid into a sterilised glass jar, add the agave syrup and gently shake to combine. This will keep for up to 3 months in a cool dry place.

# MUSHROOM AND TRUFFLE PATE

MAKES 1.25 KG (2 LB 12 OZ)

BASE
450 g (1 lb) carrots, cut into small dice
1.5 kg (3 lb 5 oz) brown onions, cut into small dice
400 g (14 oz) celery, cut into small dice
250 ml (9 fl oz/1 cup) tamari
310 ml (10¾ fl oz/1¼ cups) coconut nectar
250 ml (9 fl oz/1 cup) apple cider vinegar
500 ml (17 fl oz/2 cups) water

FLAVOUR
750 g (1 lb 10 oz) Swiss brown mushrooms, halved
560 ml (19¼ fl oz/2¼ cups) extra virgin olive oil, plus extra to store
155 g (5½ oz/1 cup) cashews
2 tablespoons truffle oil or ½ g fresh local truffle

To make the base, put the carrots, onions and celery in a large bowl. Add the tamari, coconut nectar, apple cider vinegar and water, and stir to coat the vegetables.

Line two baking trays with baking paper. Spread the carrot mixture on one of the trays. Put the mushroom halves on the other tray and place both in the dehydrator. Dehydrate the mushrooms for 10 hours, and dehydrate the carrot mixture for 20 hours.

Put the carrot mixture and mushrooms in a food processor with all the remaining flavour ingredients and process for 5 minutes. You may need to do this in batches.

Allow the mixture to cool (so it doesn't heat over 45°C/113°F) and process for another 5 minutes.

Spoon the pâté into sterilised glass jars, pour a little olive oil over the top and seal each jar with a lid. Refrigerate overnight to allow the flavours to develop.

NOTE Refrigerate for at least 12 hours for the best result.

# CARROT AND FENNEL PATE

MAKES 1 KG (2 LB 4 OZ)

BASE
450 g (1 lb) carrots, cut into small dice
1.5 kg (3 lb 5 oz) brown onions, cut into small dice
400 g (14 oz) celery, cut into small dice
250 ml (9 fl oz/1 cup) tamari
310 ml (10¾ fl oz/1¼ cups) coconut nectar
250 ml (9 fl oz/1 cup) apple cider vinegar
500 ml (17 fl oz/2 cups) water

FLAVOUR
560 ml (19¼ fl oz/2¼ cups) extra virgin olive oil, plus extra to store
1 tablespoon fennel seeds
2 teaspoons coriander seeds

To make the base, put the carrots, onions and celery in a large bowl. Add the tamari, coconut nectar, apple cider vinegar and water, and stir to coat the vegetables.

Spread the carrot mixture on a baking tray lined with baking paper and place in the dehydrator for 20 hours.

Put the carrot mixture in a food processor with all the flavour ingredients and process for 5 minutes. You may need to do this in batches.

Allow the mixture to cool (so it doesn't heat over 45°C/113°F) and process for another 5 minutes.

Spoon the pâté into sterilised glass jars, pour a little olive oil over the top and seal each jar with a lid. Refrigerate overnight to allow the flavours to develop.

NOTE Refrigerate for at least 12 hours for the best result.

# OLIVE PATE

MAKES 1.3 KG (3 LB)

BASE
450 g (1 lb) carrots, cut into small dice
1.5 kg (3 lb 5 oz) brown onions, cut into small dice
400 g (14 oz) celery, cut into small dice
250 ml (9 fl oz/1 cup) tamari
310 ml (10¾ fl oz/1¼ cups) coconut nectar
250 ml (9 fl oz/1 cup) apple cider vinegar
500 ml (17 fl oz/2 cups) water

FLAVOUR
600 g (1 lb 5 oz/4 cups) pitted Kalamata olives
560 ml (19¼ fl oz/2¼ cups) extra virgin olive oil, plus extra to store

Put the carrots, onions and celery in a large bowl. Add the tamari, coconut nectar, apple cider vinegar and water, and stir to coat the vegetables.

Line two baking trays with baking paper. Spread the carrot mixture on one of the trays. Spread the olives on the other tray, and place both trays in the dehydrator. Dehydrate the olives for 15 hours, and dehydrate the carrot mixture for 20 hours.

Put the carrot mixture and olives in a food processor with the olive oil and process for 5 minutes. You might need to do this in batches.

Allow the mixture to cool (so it doesn't heat over 45°C/113°F) and process for another 5 minutes.

Spoon the pâté into sterilised glass jars, pour a little olive oil over the top and seal each jar with a lid. Refrigerate overnight to allow the flavours to develop.

NOTE Refrigerate for at least 12 hours for the best result.

# BASIL AND KALE PESTO

MAKES 1.25 KG (2 LB 12 OZ)

120 g (4¼ oz) basil
100 g (3½ oz) kale
750 ml (26 fl oz/3 cups) extra virgin olive oil
310 g (11 oz/2 cups) cashews
125 ml (4 fl oz/½ cup) lemon juice
4 garlic cloves, grated
¼ brown onion, roughly chopped
1 tablespoon spirulina powder
1 teaspoon pink lake salt
⅓ teaspoon freshly ground black pepper

Put all the ingredients in a food processor and process for 5 minutes.

Allow the mixture to cool for 5 minutes, then pour into sterilised glass jars and refrigerate. This will keep for up to 1 month.

NOTE This pesto will be your best friend in the kitchen, as you can use it for absolutely everything, from a simple dip for carrot sticks to complicated tart recipes.

# NETTLE PESTO

MAKES 850 G (1 LB 14 OZ)

200 g (7 oz) young nettle leaves
500 ml (17 fl oz/2 cups) extra virgin olive oil
155 g (5½ oz/1 cup) cashews
125 ml (4 fl oz/½ cup) lemon juice
4 garlic cloves, grated
¼ brown onion, roughly chopped
1 teaspoon pink lake salt
⅓ teaspoon freshly ground black pepper

It's a good idea to wear gloves when handling nettles. Carefully place the nettle leaves in a medium bowl. Bring a kettle of water to the boil, allow to cool for 5 minutes, then pour over the nettle leaves. Cover the bowl with a chopping board for 5 minutes before draining the leaves through a fine sieve.

Put the drained nettle leaves and all the other ingredients in a food processor and process for 5 minutes.

Allow the mixture to cool for 5 minutes, then pour into sterilised glass jars and refrigerate. This will keep for up to 2 weeks.

# MUSHROOM PEPPERBERRY SAUCE

MAKES 1.2 KG (2 LB 10 OZ)

250 g (9 oz) Swiss brown mushrooms, halved
750 ml (26 fl oz/3 cups) extra virgin olive oil
155 g (5½ oz/1 cup) cashews
125 ml (4 fl oz/½ cup) lemon juice
4 garlic cloves, grated
¼ brown onion, roughly chopped
1 tablespoon pepperberries
1 teaspoon pink lake salt
⅓ teaspoon freshly ground black pepper

Put the mushrooms in a medium bowl, add 125 ml (4 fl oz/½ cup) of olive oil and stir to coat.

Spread the mushrooms out on a baking tray lined with baking paper. Place the tray in the dehydrator and dehydrate for 18 hours.

After dehydration, put the mushrooms and the remaining ingredients in a food processor and process for 5 minutes. Allow the mixture to cool for 5 minutes.

Separate the mixture into two batches. Pour one batch into a high-speed blender and blend for 20 seconds. Repeat with the other half.

Allow the mixture to cool for 5 minutes, then pour into sterilised glass jars and refrigerate. This will keep for up to 1 month.

NOTE This sauce goes well with any earthy vegetables, such as carrots, beetroot (beets), hardy lettuce or even on mushrooms.

# WALNUT BOLOGNESE

MAKES 1.2 KG (2 LB 10 OZ)

650 g (1 lb 7 oz) tomatoes
500 ml (17 fl oz/2 cups) extra virgin olive oil
80 g (2¾ oz/½ cup) cashews
60 ml (2 fl oz/¼ cup) lemon juice
2 garlic cloves, grated
¼ brown onion, roughly chopped
½ teaspoon pink lake salt
⅓ teaspoon freshly ground black pepper
70 g (2½ oz/½ cup) walnut pieces

Cut the tomatoes into quarters and spread them on a baking tray lined with baking paper. Place the baking tray in the dehydrator for 20 hours.

After dehydration, put the tomatoes, olive oil, cashews, lemon juice, garlic, onion, salt and pepper into a food processor and process for 5 minutes.

Allow to cool for 5 minutes, then add the walnuts and process for 10 seconds.

Allow to cool for 5 minutes, then pour into sterilised glass jars and refrigerate. This will keep for up to 1 month.

# SPICY TOMATO RELISH

MAKES 1 KG (2 LB 4 OZ)

650 g (1 lb 7 oz) tomatoes
500 ml (17 fl oz/2 cups) extra virgin olive oil
60 ml (2 fl oz/¼ cup) lemon juice
4 garlic cloves, grated
¼ brown onion, roughly chopped
½ teaspoon pink lake salt
⅓ teaspoon freshly ground black pepper
1 teaspoon ground cumin

Cut the tomatoes into quarters and spread out on a baking tray lined with baking paper. Place the baking tray in the dehydrator and dehydrate for 8 hours.

Put the tomatoes and all the other ingredients in a food processor and process for 20 seconds.

Allow to cool for 5 minutes, then pour into sterilised glass jars and refrigerate. This will keep for up to 1 month.

# VANILLA BEAN PASTE

MAKES 1.5 KG (3 LB 5 OZ)

500 g (1 lb 2 oz) vanilla beans
1 litre (35 fl oz/4 cups) coconut nectar
250 ml (9 fl oz/1 cup) rum

Put half of each ingredient in a blender and blend on high for 4 minutes, stopping for about 20 seconds after each minute. Repeat with the remaining ingredients.

Store in sterilised glass jars in the refrigerator. This will keep for up to 3 months.

NOTE This recipe makes quite a large batch, but it's an important staple for many of the dishes in this book, and you'll find you'll go through it quickly.

# CHOCOLATE SAUCE

MAKES 370 ML (12½ FL OZ)

100 g (3½ oz/1 cup) cacao powder, sifted
250 ml (9 fl oz/1 cup) coconut nectar
1 tablespoon orange juice
½ teaspoon vanilla bean paste (above)
½ teaspoon vanilla salt (page 103)

Put all the ingredients in a blender and blend for 1 minute.

Pour into a sterilised glass jar and store in a cool dry place. This will keep for up to 3 months.

# AGENT SIX PRALINE

MAKES 870 G (1 LB 15 OZ)

155 g (5½ oz/1 cup) cashews
250 ml (9 fl oz/1 cup) water
250 ml (9 fl oz/1 cup) coconut nectar
1 teaspoon vanilla bean paste (opposite)
½ teaspoon vanilla salt (page 103)
1 tablespoon coconut oil, melted
½ teaspoon cacao butter, melted
½ teaspoon extra virgin olive oil
100 g (3½ oz/1 cup) cacao powder, sifted
75 g (2½ oz/½ cup) hazelnuts, crushed

Put the cashews and water in a blender and blend until smooth.

Add the coconut nectar, vanilla bean paste and vanilla salt, and blend for a further 10 seconds.

Add the coconut oil, cacao butter and olive oil. Blend for another 5 seconds, then add the cacao powder and blend on low until thoroughly mixed.

Add the hazelnuts and gently stir through. Pour into sterilised glass jars and store in the refrigerator. This will keep for up to 1 month.

# SALTED CARAMEL

MAKES 500 G (1 LB 2 OZ)

250 ml (9 fl oz/1 cup) coconut nectar
80 g (2¾ oz/½ cup) cashews
125 ml (4 fl oz/½ cup) freshly brewed coffee
1 tablespoon cacao butter, melted
1 tablespoon vanilla bean paste (page 118)
½ teaspoon vanilla salt (page 103)

Put all the ingredients in a blender and blend on low for 2 minutes, then increase the speed to high and blend for 5 minutes.

Pour into sterilised glass jars and allow to cool before putting the lids on. Store in a cool dry place for up to 2 weeks.

When ready to use, put the jar in the dehydrator with the lid open for 30 minutes to soften.


# COFFEE SYRUP

MAKES 700 ML (24 FL OZ)

500 ml (17 fl oz/2 cups) freshly brewed coffee
60 ml (2 fl oz/¼ cup) rum
125 ml (4 fl oz/½ cup) coconut nectar
2 teaspoons extra virgin olive oil
1 teaspoon guar gum

Put all the ingredients in a blender and blend on very low speed for 10 seconds until well combined.

Pour into sterilised glass jars and store in the refrigerator. This will keep for up to 2 weeks.

NOTE This coffee syrup has a complementary mix of ingredients, which gives it depth and richness.

# CITRUS DRESSING

MAKES 330 ML (11¼ FL OZ/1⅓ CUPS)

250 ml (9 fl oz/1 cup) extra virgin olive oil
80 ml (2½ fl oz/⅓ cup) lemon juice
1 tablespoon lime juice
1 teaspoon pink lake salt
⅓ teaspoon freshly ground black pepper

Put all the ingredients in a sterilised glass jar, put the lid on and shake well. Use immediately or refrigerate for up to 1 week.


# WALNUT DRESSING

MAKES 430 ML (14½ FL OZ)

250 ml (9 fl oz/1 cup) walnut oil
60 ml (2 fl oz/¼ cup) extra virgin olive oil
60 ml (2 fl oz/¼ cup) grape seed oil
60 ml (2 fl oz/¼ cup) lime juice
1 teaspoon pink lake salt
⅓ teaspoon freshly ground black pepper

Put all the ingredients in a sterilised glass jar, put the lid on and shake well. Use immediately or refrigerate for up to 1 week.

# HORSERADISH DRESSING

MAKES 350 ML (12 FL OZ)

250 ml (9 fl oz/1 cup) extra virgin olive oil
60 ml (2 fl oz/¼ cup) apple cider vinegar
1 tablespoon lime juice
2 tablespoons freshly grated horseradish
1 teaspoon pink lake salt
⅓ teaspoon freshly ground black pepper

Put all the ingredients in a sterilised glass jar, put the lid on and shake well. Use immediately or refrigerate for up to 1 week.

# SESAME DRESSING

MAKES 250 ML (9 FL OZ/1 CUP)

125 ml (4 fl oz/½ cup) extra virgin olive oil
60 ml (2 fl oz/¼ cup) sesame oil
60 ml (2 fl oz/¼ cup) apple cider vinegar
2 tablespoons tamari
1 teaspoon pink lake salt
⅓ teaspoon freshly ground black pepper

Put all the ingredients in a sterilised glass jar, put the lid on and shake well. Use immediately or refrigerate for up to 1 week.

# MISO DRESSING

MAKES 300 ML (10¼ FL OZ)

125 ml (4 fl oz/½ cup) extra virgin olive oil
60 ml (2 fl oz/¼ cup) sesame oil
60 ml (2 fl oz/¼ cup) miso
60 ml (2 fl oz/¼ cup) apple cider vinegar
1 tablespoon tamari
⅓ teaspoon freshly ground black pepper

Put all the ingredients in a sterilised glass jar, put the lid on and shake well. Use immediately or refrigerate for up to 1 week.

# CASHEW YOGHURT DRESSING

MAKES 340 ML (11½ FL OZ)

260 g (9¼ oz/1 cup) cashew yoghurt (page 75)
60 ml (2 fl oz/¼ cup) extra virgin olive oil
1 tablespoon apple cider vinegar
1 teaspoon pink lake salt
⅓ teaspoon freshly ground black pepper

Put all the ingredients in a sterilised glass jar, put the lid on and shake well. Use immediately or refrigerate for up to 1 week.

# CREAMY DRESSING

MAKES 320 ML (10¾ FL OZ)

200 g (7 oz/1 cup) classic cashew cheese (page 80)
60 ml (2 fl oz/¼ cup) extra virgin olive oil
60 ml (2 fl oz/¼ cup) apple cider vinegar
1 tablespoon tamari
1 teaspoon pink lake salt
⅓ teaspoon freshly ground black pepper

Put all the ingredients in a sterilised glass jar, put the lid on and shake well. Use immediately or refrigerate for up to 1 week.

# BALSAMIC DRESSING

MAKES 330 ML (11¼ FL OZ/1⅓ CUPS)

250 ml (9 fl oz/1 cup) extra virgin olive oil
60 ml (2 fl oz/¼ cup) balsamic vinegar
1 tablespoon port
½ teaspoon pink lake salt
⅓ teaspoon freshly ground black pepper

Put all the ingredients in a sterilised glass jar, put the lid on and shake well. Use immediately or refrigerate for up to 1 week.

# SWEET DRESSING

MAKES 410 ML (14 FL OZ)

250 ml (9 fl oz/1 cup) extra virgin olive oil
60 ml (2 fl oz/¼ cup) lemon juice
80 ml (2½ fl oz/⅓ cup) coconut nectar
1 tablespoon tamari
½ teaspoon pink lake salt
⅓ teaspoon freshly ground black pepper

Put all the ingredients in a sterilised glass jar, put the lid on and shake well. Use immediately or refrigerate for up to 1 week.

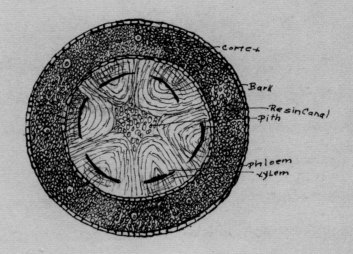

Cortex
Bark
Resin Canal
Pith
Phloem
Xylem

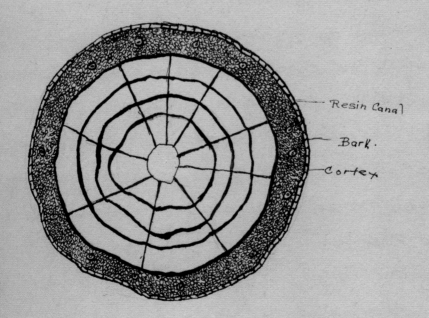

Resin Canal
Bark.
Cortex

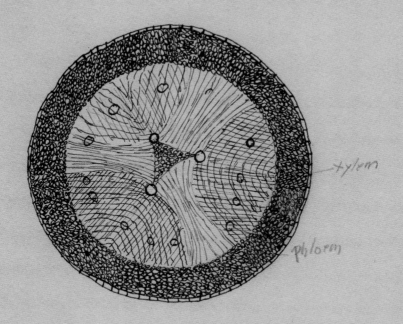

xylem

phloem

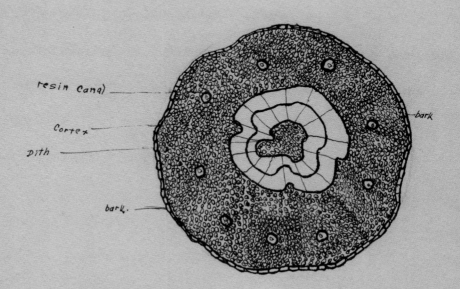

resin canal

cortex

pith

bark

bark.

recipes

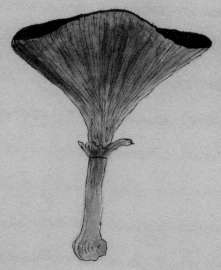

# breakfast

Single Flower
(Female)

Corolla

Pistil

Ovary

Fruit (feathered achene)

# 'POACHED' PEAR WITH YOGHURT

FOR 4

2 beurre bosc pears, or pears of choice
260 g (9¼ oz/1 cup) cashew yoghurt (page 75)
30 g (1 oz/¼ cup) pistachio kernels, crushed
micro mint, to serve (optional)

POACHING LIQUID
1 litre (35 fl oz/4 cups) young Thai coconut water
125 ml (4 fl oz/½ cup) coconut nectar
2 tablespoons lucuma powder
2 tablespoons rum
zest of 1 orange
1 vanilla bean
1 star anise
1 cinnamon stick
¼ teaspoon vanilla salt (page 103)

To prepare the poaching liquid, combine the ingredients in a large bowl.

Peel the pears, keeping the stems intact, and cut a small slice from the base of each pear so they can sit upright without toppling. Place the pears in the poaching liquid. To keep the pears submerged, cut a circle of baking paper the size of the bowl and set it on the surface of the liquid. Place a small plate on top of the paper so it keeps the pears in the liquid. Freeze for 10 hours.

Remove from the freezer and place in the dehydrator for 2 hours to defrost.

Transfer the pears and liquid from the bowl into a shallow baking tray lined with baking paper. Place the tray in the dehydrator for 24 hours.

Halve the pears. Divide the cashew yoghurt between four bowls and top with half a pear, the crushed pistachios and micro mint (if using).

# PEAR AND MUSCATEL CANELES

MAKES 6-8 MUFFINS OR CANELES

60 ml (2 fl oz/¼ cup) coconut oil, melted
310 g (11 oz/2 cups) cashews
60 ml (2 fl oz/¼ cup) cashew milk (page 74)
35 g (1¼ oz/¼ cup) coconut sugar
85 g (3 oz/¼ cup) pear and muscatel jam (page 94)
35 g (1¼ oz/¼ cup) cacao nibs
25 g (1 oz/¼ cup) cacao powder

Use 1½ tablespoons of the coconut oil to grease six to eight canelé moulds or six to eight holes in a mini muffin tray.

Put the remaining oil and the rest of the ingredients in a large bowl and mix well.

Spoon the mixture into the moulds and place in the dehydrator for 16 hours. Cool in the moulds.

Remove the canelés or muffins from the moulds or muffin tray by gently loosening with a small thin-bladed knife.

# 'STEWED' PLUM

FOR 4

1 kg (2 lb 4 oz) sour plums
1 litre (35 fl oz/4 cups) cinnamon orange agave syrup (page 109)

Combine the plums and cinnamon orange agave syrup in a large bowl and sit at room temperature for 5 hours.

Spread the plums and liquid on a baking tray lined with baking paper and cover with another layer of baking paper. Weight the paper down to ensure the fan in the dehydrator doesn't dislodge the paper. Dehydrate for 8 hours, remove the top layer of baking paper and then dehydrate for a further 8 hours to allow plums to caramelise.

Pour the stewed plums into sterilised glass jars and refrigerate for 12 hours. These will keep in the refrigerator for about 2 weeks.

NOTE If you're lucky enough to have a plum tree at your disposal, pick your plums 1–2 weeks early for the best sour flavour. If not, Middle Eastern grocery stores often stock sour plums.

# CHOCOLATE GRANOLA

FOR 4

155 g (5½ oz/1 cup) cashews
35 g (1¼ oz/¼ cup) walnut pieces
30 g (1 oz/¼ cup) pistachio kernels
25 g (1 oz/¼ cup) cacao powder
35 g (1¼ oz/¼ cup) cacao nibs
60 ml (2 fl oz/¼ cup) coconut nectar
2 tablespoons lucuma powder
500 ml (17 fl oz/2 cups) cashew milk (page 74)

Put the nuts, cacao powder, cacao nibs, coconut nectar and lucuma powder in a large bowl and mix thoroughly.

Spread the chocolate mixture on a baking tray lined with baking paper and place the tray in the dehydrator for 4 hours.

Break the granola up and divide between four bowls. Pour the cashew milk over to serve.

139

# BIRCHER MUESLI

FOR 4

500 ml (17 fl oz/2 cups) cashew milk (page 74)
140 g (5 oz/1 cup) walnut pieces
140 g (5 oz/1 cup) pistachio kernels
½ apple, peeled, cored and diced
1 tablespoon mesquite powder
1 teaspoon vanilla bean paste (page 118)
¼ teaspoon vanilla salt (page 103)
35 g (1¼ oz/¼ cup) cacao nibs
1 tablespoon micro shiso (optional)

Put the cashew milk, nuts, apple, mesquite powder, vanilla bean paste and vanilla salt in a food processor and process for 5 seconds.

Divide the mixture between four bowls and sprinkle with the cacao nibs and micro shiso (if using).

NOTE You can add less cashew milk if you prefer a thicker, more traditional consistency.

# CHIA PORRIDGE WITH MESQUITE CRUMBLE

FOR 4

CHIA PORRIDGE
500 ml (17 fl oz/2 cups) young Thai coconut water
35 g (1¼ oz/¼ cup) coconut sugar
1 teaspoon vanilla bean paste (page 118)
1 teaspoon rosewater
½ teaspoon vanilla salt (page 103)
35 g (1¼ oz/¼ cup) chia seeds

MESQUITE CRUMBLE
2 x sweet tart bases (page 105), made with an extra 1 tablespoon mesquite powder

To prepare the chia porridge, put the coconut water, coconut sugar, vanilla bean paste, rosewater and vanilla salt in a blender and blend for 10 seconds.

Pour the coconut mixture into a medium bowl, add the chia seeds and whisk gently to combine. Refrigerate for 1 hour.

For the mesquite crumble, break the sweet tart bases into small pieces.

To serve, divide the porridge between four bowls and top with the crumble.

# STRAWBERRY AND PEPPERBERRY CRUMBLE

FOR 4

2 x sweet tart bases (page 105)
80 g (2¾ oz/¼ cup) strawberry and pepperberry jam (page 92)
80 g (2¾ oz) vanilla cashew cream (page 74)

Crumble the sweet tart bases and divide between four small bowls. Top each with a quarter of the jam and cream.

# DEHYDRATED TOMATO LABNEH

FOR 4

260 g (9¼ oz/1 cup) cashew yoghurt (page 75)
6 dehydrated tomatoes (page 57), chopped
2 Lebanese cucumbers, chopped
4 Thai mint sprigs, torn
80 ml (2½ fl oz/⅓ cup) lime juice
1 tablespoon pink lake salt

Line a colander with muslin (cheesecloth) and place over a medium bowl. Place the cashew yoghurt on the muslin and wrap the muslin over the yoghurt to enclose. Place a weight on top. Refrigerate for 2 hours.

Remove the yoghurt from the muslin and spoon into a medium bowl. Add the remaining ingredients and mix to combine.

NOTE This tomato labneh is great by itself, or serve it with a savoury tart.

# CRUMBLE WITH BLACK FOREST COMPOTE AND FRENCH VANILLA ICE-CREAM

FOR 4

2 x sweet tart bases (page 105)
320 g (11¼ oz/1 cup) black forest compote (page 99)
50 g (1¾ oz/⅓ cup) French vanilla ice-cream (page 85)

Crumble the sweet tart bases and divide between four bowls. Top each with a quarter of the compote and ice-cream.

# CUMQUAT AND BRANDY MARMALADE WITH MASCARPONE TART

FOR 4

4 x sweet tart bases (page 105)
120 g (4¼ oz/½ cup) cashew mascarpone (page 84)
115 g (4 oz/⅓ cup) cumquat and brandy marmalade (page 96)

Top each of the tart bases with a quarter of the cashew mascarpone and cumquat and brandy marmalade.

tarts

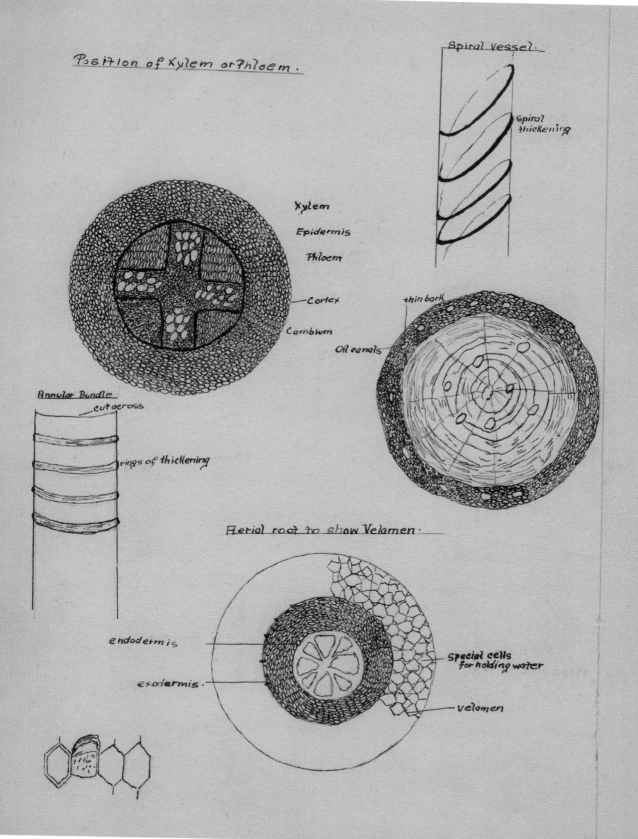

Position of Xylem or Phloem.

Spiral Vessel.

Spiral thickening

Xylem

Epidermis

Phloem

Cortex

Cambium

thin bark

Oil canals

Annular Bundle

cut across

rings of thickening

Aerial root to show Velamen.

endodermis

exodermis.

special cells for holding water

Velamen

# CLASSIC CASHEW CHEESE TARTS

FOR 4

200 g (7 oz/1 cup) classic cashew cheese (page 80)
4 x savoury tart bases (page 105)
1 handful sea spray (sea blite) or wild rocket (arugula)

Gently spread the classic cashew cheese on the tart bases, then top with the sea spray or wild rocket.

NOTE Serve with sea spray if you'd like to bring out the salty flavour from the classic cashew cheese. If you would like to enhance the peppery flavour of the cheese, use the wild rocket.

# BABY LEEK TARTS

FOR 4

125 g (4½ oz/½ cup) cashew mayonnaise (page 77)
4 x savoury tart bases (page 105)
1 cup dehydrated leeks (page 58)
micro lemon balm, to serve

Gently spread a quarter of the cashew mayonnaise on each tart base and top with the dehydrated baby leeks and micro lemon balm.

# LEMON AND DILL CHEESE TARTS WITH PEA AND MUSHROOM

FOR 4

75 g (2½ oz/½ cup) frozen peas
200 g (7 oz/1 cup) lemon and dill cashew cheese (page 81)
1 cup dehydrated fennel bulbs (page 56), chopped (optional)
4 x savoury tart bases (page 105)
1 cup dehydrated mushrooms (page 55)


Put the peas in a colander and rinse under warm water for 1 minute.

Gently combine the peas, lemon and dill cashew cheese and fennel in a large bowl.

Spread a quarter of the cheese mixture on each tart base and garnish with the dehydrated mushrooms. Serve immediately.

# GARLIC AND CHIVE CHEESE TARTS WITH GARLIC AND TOMATO

FOR 4

200 g (7 oz/1 cup) garlic and chive cashew cheese (page 83)
4 dehydrated garlic cloves (page 62), skin removed and thinly sliced,
plus extra for garnish (optional)
4 x savoury tart bases (page 105)
4 dehydrated tomatoes (page 57)

Gently combine the garlic and chive cashew cheese and garlic in a medium bowl.

Spread a quarter of the cheese mixture on each tart base and place a tomato on top of each.

Garnish with dehydrated garlic (if desired). Serve immediately.

# OYSTER MUSHROOM TARTS WITH MUSHROOM AND TRUFFLE PATE

FOR 4

100 g (3½ oz/½ cup) classic cashew cheese (page 80)
4 x savoury tart bases (page 105)
65 g (2¼ oz/⅓ cup) mushroom and truffle pâté (page 110)
½ cup dehydrated oyster mushrooms (page 55)

Gently spread a quarter of the classic cashew cheese on each tart base. Swirl a tablespoon of mushroom and truffle pâté in the centre of each and top with the mushrooms.

# BABY ROOT VEGETABLE TARTS WITH CARROT AND FENNEL PATE

FOR 4

200 g (7 oz/1 cup) classic cashew cheese (page 80)
4 x savoury tart bases (page 105)
65 g (2¼ oz/⅓ cup) carrot and fennel pâté (page 111)
4 dehydrated baby beetroot (beets) (page 63)
4 dehydrated baby heirloom carrots (page 54)
4 dehydrated Dutch carrots, parsnips or turnips (use same method as the dehydrated baby beetroot) (page 63)

Gently spread a quarter of the classic cashew cheese on each tart base. Place a tablespoon of carrot and fennel pâté in the centre of each and top with the root vegetables.

NOTE You can be as creative as you like with this tart recipe. Use onions, leeks, garlic and any other root vegetables - whatever is in season.

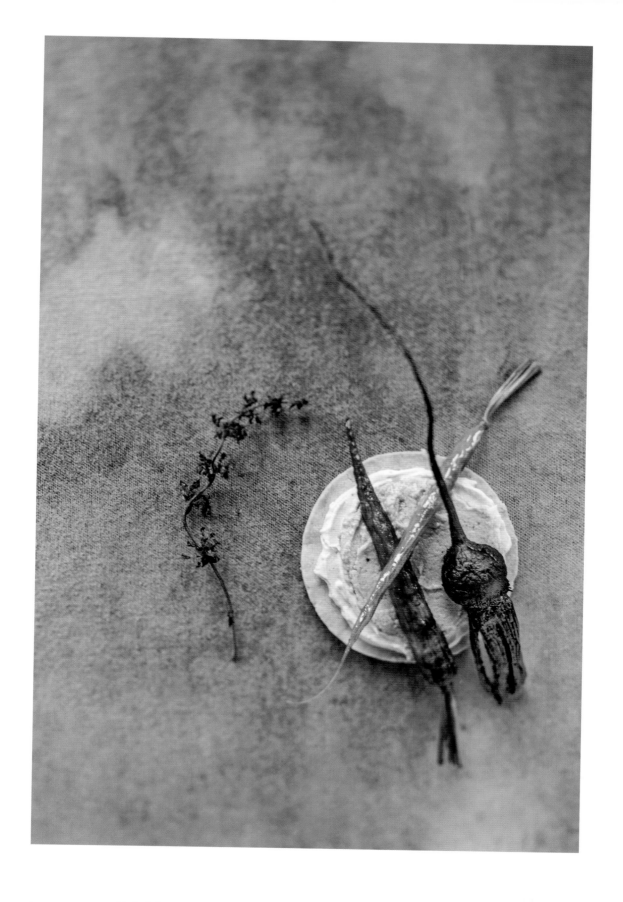

# VANILLA PEACH JAM AND COCONUT SEMIFREDDO TARTS

FOR 4

240 g (8½ oz/1 cup) coconut semifreddo (page 241)
4 x sweet tart bases (page 105)
115 g (4 oz/⅓ cup) vanilla peach jam (page 93), stones discarded

Divide the coconut semifreddo between the tart bases and top each with a tablespoon of jam.

# FIG JAM AND CASHEW MASCARPONE TARTS

FOR 4

240 g (8½ oz/1 cup) cashew mascarpone (page 84)
4 x sweet tart bases (page 105)
115 g (4 oz/⅓ cup) fig jam (page 95)

Gently spread a quarter of the cashew mascarpone on each tart base and top with a tablespoon of fig jam.

# AGENT SIX PRALINE TARTS WITH GLAZED ORANGES AND MINT SLICE ICE-CREAM

FOR 4

60 g (2¼ oz/¼ cup) agent six praline (page 119)

4 x sweet tart bases (page 105)

85 g (3 oz/¼ cup) saffron orange marmalade (page 97)

50 g (1¾ oz/⅓ cup) mint slice ice-cream (page 242)

crushed cacao beans to serve (optional)

Divide the praline between the tart bases. Remove the glazed orange pieces from the marmalade (the syrup won't be used). Divide the orange pieces and ice-cream between the four tarts and sprinkle with crushed cacao beans (if using).

Serve immediately.

# WILD VICTORIAN BLUEBERRY YOGHURT TARTS

FOR 4

200 g (7 oz/1 cup) cashew yoghurt (page 75)
4 x sweet tart bases (page 105)
35 g (1¼ oz/¼ cup) coconut sugar
1 teaspoon mesquite powder
155 g (5½ oz/1 cup) blueberries

Gently spread a quarter of the cashew yoghurt on each tart base. Combine the coconut sugar and mesquite powder in a small mixing bowl. Top each tart with blueberries and sprinkle the coconut sugar mixture on top.

soups

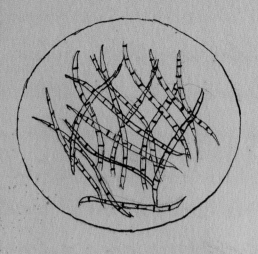

spirogyra
under
low power.

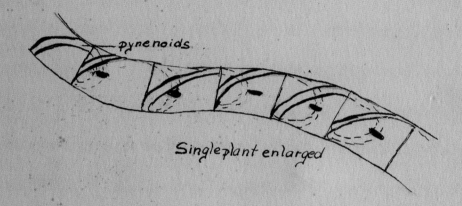

pyrenoids

Single plant enlarged

Single cell

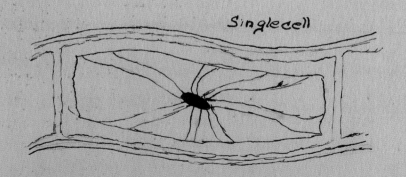

# PEA, DILL AND MINT SOUP

FOR 4

280 g (10 oz/2 cups) frozen peas
500 ml (17 fl oz/2 cups) young Thai coconut water
170 g (6 oz/1 cup) young Thai coconut meat
1 large handful dill, about 25 g (1 oz)
1 handful mint leaves
60 ml (2 fl oz/¼ cup) lime juice
60 ml (2 fl oz/¼ cup) extra virgin olive oil
2 garlic cloves, grated
1 French shallot, grated
1 teaspoon tamari
1 teaspoon pink lake salt
1 teaspoon freshly ground black pepper

Blend all the ingredients in a blender for 10 seconds.

Divide the soup between four bowls and serve immediately.

# BABY LEEK BROTH WITH NETTLE PESTO AND DEHYDRATED NETTLE LEAVES

FOR 4

10 nettle leaves
80 ml (2½ fl oz/⅓ cup) extra virgin olive oil
½ teaspoon pink lake salt
1 litre (35 fl oz/4 cups) young Thai coconut water
2 cups dehydrated baby leeks (page 58), double batch needed
2 garlic cloves, grated
1 French shallot, grated
1 tablespoon tamari
80 g (2¾ oz/⅓ cup) nettle pesto (page 114)

Put the nettle leaves in a small bowl. Boil some water and then allow it to cool for 5 minutes before pouring the water over the nettle leaves. Set aside for 2 minutes.

Remove the nettle leaves from the hot water, taking care not to burn yourself, and place them on a baking tray lined with baking paper. Drizzle the leaves with 2 tablespoons of the olive oil and sprinkle with the salt. Place the tray in the dehydrator for 2 hours.

Put the coconut water, leeks, garlic, shallot and tamari in a blender with the remaining olive oil and blend for 2 minutes.

Divide the broth, nettle leaves and nettle pesto between four bowls.

# THAI BROTH WITH 'RICE' NOODLES

FOR 4

1 litre (35 fl oz/4 cups) young Thai coconut water
2 celery stalks, chopped
2 spring onions (scallions), chopped
1 French shallot, grated
2 garlic cloves, grated
2 tablespoons sesame oil
2 zucchini (courgettes)
½ teaspoon pink lake salt
4 red radishes
1 small handful Thai basil leaves

Blend the coconut water, celery, spring onions, shallot, garlic and 1 tablespoon of the sesame oil in a blender for 1 minute.

Cut the zucchini thinly into ribbons and combine with the remaining sesame oil and the salt in a medium bowl. Set aside for 5 minutes for the ribbons to soften.

Thinly slice the red radishes and set aside.

Divide the liquid between four soup bowls and add a quarter each of the zucchini and radishes. Top with the basil leaves.

THAI BROTH WITH 'RICE' NOODLES

177

CREAMY MUSHROOM AND PEPPERBERRY SOUP

# CREAMY MUSHROOM AND PEPPERBERRY SOUP

FOR 4

1 litre (35 fl oz/4 cups) young Thai coconut water
340 g (12 oz/2 cups) young Thai coconut meat
1½ cups mushroom pepperberry sauce (page 115)

Blend all the ingredients in a blender for 1 minute.

Divide the soup between four bowls and serve.


# WILD MUSHROOM CHOWDER

FOR 4

1 litre (35 fl oz/4 cups) young Thai coconut water
4 cups dehydrated mushrooms (page 55)
2 garlic cloves, grated
1 French shallot, grated
1 tablespoon tamari
2 tablespoons sesame oil
1 tablespoon extra virgin olive oil
½ teaspoon pink lake salt

Blend all the ingredients in a blender for 1 minute.

Divide the soup between four bowls and enjoy.


NOTE If you would like to add some extra texture, leave a whole mushroom aside to go into your soup – slice, chop or leave whole, depending on your preferred texture.

# CARROT AND PISTACHIO SOUP

FOR 4

1 litre (35 fl oz/4 cups) young Thai coconut water
190 g (6¾ oz/1 cup) carrot and fennel pâté (page 111)
2 tablespoons extra virgin olive oil
½ teaspoon freshly ground black pepper
140 g (5 oz/1 cup) pistachio kernels, chopped

Blend the coconut water, pâté, olive oil and pepper in a blender for 2 minutes.

Divide the soup between four bowls, sprinkle with the pistachios and serve.

NOTE This soup can be served chilled, at room temperature or placed in the dehydrator to warm up.

# TOMATO GAZPACHO WITH SAFFRON OIL

FOR 4

24 small tomatoes
125 ml (4 fl oz/½ cup) extra virgin olive oil
60 ml (2 fl oz/¼ cup) apple cider vinegar
1 teaspoon saffron threads
1 teaspoon freshly ground black pepper

Put the tomatoes in a blender (you might need to do this in batches) and blend for 3 minutes.

Pour the tomato purée into a muslin- (cheesecloth-) lined colander, set over a large bowl and refrigerate, covered, for 24 hours.

Put the olive oil, apple cider vinegar and saffron in a blender and blend for 10 seconds. Set aside until needed.

Discard the tomato pulp remaining in the colander. Divide the strained tomato gazpacho between four bowls. Sprinkle the black pepper and drizzle the saffron oil over the top of each bowl and serve immediately.

# MUSHROOM AND TRUFFLE SOUP

FOR 4

1 litre (35 fl oz/4 cups) young Thai coconut water
190 g (6¾ oz/1 cup) mushroom and truffle pâté (page 110)

Blend all the ingredients in a blender for 1 minute.

Divide the soup between four bowls and serve.

# SWEET CORN SOUP WITH YOUNG THAI COCONUT CREAM

FOR 4

1 litre (35 fl oz/4 cups) young Thai coconut water
510 g (1 lb 2 oz/3 cups) young Thai coconut meat
800 g (1 lb 12 oz/4 cups) fresh corn kernels; alternatively, use 600 g (1 lb 5 oz/4 cups)
    frozen corn kernels
1 carrot, roughly chopped
1 celery stalk, roughly chopped
1 French shallot, grated
2 tablespoons extra virgin olive oil

Blend all the ingredients in a blender for 1 minute.

Divide the soup between four bowls and enjoy.


# SPICY TOMATO AND STRAWBERRY SOUP

FOR 4

1 litre (35 fl oz/4 cups) young Thai coconut water
340 g (12 oz/2 cups) young Thai coconut meat
410 g (14½ oz/2 cups) spicy tomato relish (page 117), double batch needed
500 g (1 lb 2 oz/3⅓ cups) strawberries, hulled

Blend all the ingredients in a blender for 2 minutes.

Divide the soup between four bowls and serve.

salads

Prothallus.

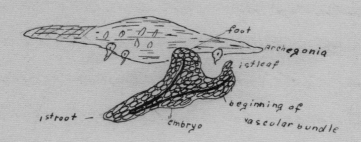

foot

archegonia

1st leaf

beginning of
vascular bundle

1st root —

embryo

Young Plant

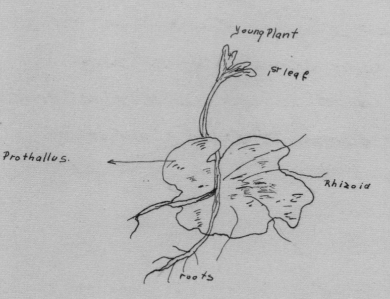

1st leaf

Prothallus.

Rhizoid

roots

# OLIVE CRUST WITH TOMATO RELISH AND CASHEW CHEESE

FOR 4

340 g (12 oz/2 cups) young Thai coconut meat
2 cups dehydrated black olives (page 58)
60 ml (2 fl oz/¼ cup) water
50 g (1¾ oz/¼ cup) classic cashew cheese (page 80)
50 g (1¾ oz/¼ cup) spicy tomato relish (page 117)
1 small handful micro Thai basil
1 small handful micro Thai mint

Place the coconut meat, olives and water in a blender and blend for 3 minutes.

Spread the olive mixture on a baking tray lined with baking paper and place the tray into a dehydrator for 20 hours.

Serve the olive crust with dollops of the cashew cheese and tomato relish, and the herbs scattered over the top.

# BABY BEETROOT, CARROTS AND LEEKS WITH WITLOF

FOR 4

8 witlof (chicory)
4 dehydrated baby beetroot (beets) (page 63)
4 dehydrated baby heirloom carrots (page 54)
1 dehydrated baby leek (page 58)
80 ml (2½ oz/⅓ cup) walnut dressing (page 121)
45 g (1½ oz/⅓ cup) walnut pieces, gently crushed

Dehydrate the witlof for 30 minutes using the same method as used for the dehydrated carrots (page 54).

Divide the dehydrated vegetables between four plates and top each with a quarter of the walnut dressing and crushed walnut pieces.

# ASPARAGUS WITH MAYONNAISE AND TAMARI

FOR 4

12 asparagus spears
80 g (2¾ oz) cashew mayonnaise (page 77)
2 tablespoons tamari

Bring some water to the boil and allow to cool for 5 minutes. Place the asparagus in a large bowl and pour over enough of the hot water to cover them completely. Place a chopping board over the bowl and leave for 5 minutes. Drain and allow to cool.

Combine the mayonnaise and tamari in a small bowl and toss with the asparagus.

Divide the dressed asparagus between four plates and serve.

# TORN LETTUCE WITH MANGO AND DEHYDRATED MUSHROOMS

FOR 4

535 g (1 lb 3 oz) chopped mango flesh, about 2 mangoes
2 butter (Boston) lettuces, roughly torn
2 cups dehydrated mushrooms (page 55)
100 g (3½ oz/1 cup) sliced snow peas (home grown if possible)
50 g (1¾ oz/¼ cup) classic cashew cheese (page 80)
1 tablespoon citrus dressing (page 121)

Using your hands, gently combine all the ingredients in a large bowl.

Divide the salad between four bowls to serve.

# RED KALE, FENNEL AND TARRAGON WITH LEMON AND DILL CHEESE

FOR 4

1 bunch red kale or purple cabbage, thinly sliced
1 large handful dill or Vietnamese mint, about 20 g (¾ oz)
65 g (2¼ oz/⅓ cup) lemon and dill cashew cheese (page 81)
80 ml (2½ fl oz/⅓ cup) sesame dressing (page 122)
3 dehydrated fennel bulbs (page 56)
2 tarragon sprigs, chopped

Combine all the ingredients in a large bowl.

Divide the salad between four plates and serve.

ALTERNATIVE If you can't find red kale, the green variety is fine to use - it's much more common and has all the same health benefits.


# WATERCRESS AND DEHYDRATED TOMATOES WITH CLASSIC CASHEW CHEESE

FOR 4

120 g (4¼ oz/4 cups) picked watercress leaves
6 dehydrated tomatoes (page 57), halved
65 g (2¼ oz/⅓ cup) classic cashew cheese (page 80)
80 ml (2½ fl oz/⅓ cup) miso dressing (page 123)

Divide the watercress between four plates, top each plate with tomato and dollops of the classic cashew cheese, and drizzle with the miso dressing.

# ASPARAGUS, CUCUMBER, HONEYDEW MELON AND PEA SHOOTS WITH SWEET DRESSING

FOR 4

12 asparagus spears
6 baby cucumbers, sliced
½ cup diced micro honeydew melon or honeydew melon
30 g (1 oz/½ cup) pea shoots
60 ml (2 fl oz/¼ cup) sweet dressing (page 125)

Bring some water to the boil and allow to cool for 5 minutes.

Place the asparagus spears in a large bowl and pour over enough hot water to cover them completely. Place a chopping board over the bowl and leave for 5 minutes.

Drain and allow to cool. Combine the asparagus with the remaining ingredients in a large bowl and mix well.

Divide the salad between four plates and serve.


# CHOPPED BABY SPINACH AND FRESH TOMATO SALAD

FOR 4

150 g (5½ oz) baby English spinach leaves
2 tomatoes
¼ cup dehydrated garlic cloves (page 62)
¼ cup dehydrated olives (page 58)
60 ml (2 fl oz/¼ cup) citrus dressing (page 121)

Roughly chop the spinach and tomato, and put them in a large bowl with the remaining ingredients.

Use your hands to gently combine and divide the salad between four bowls. Serve immediately.

# MICRO DILL, CHINESE CABBAGE, RADISH AND MINT SALAD

FOR 4

½ Chinese cabbage (wong bok), sliced
4 red radishes, sliced
4 mint sprigs, torn
4 coriander (cilantro) sprigs, torn
1 small handful micro dill or dill leaves
60 ml (2 fl oz/¼ cup) citrus dressing (page 121)

Combine the cabbage, radishes, mint, coriander and dill in a medium bowl with the dressing.

Divide the salad between four plates and serve immediately.

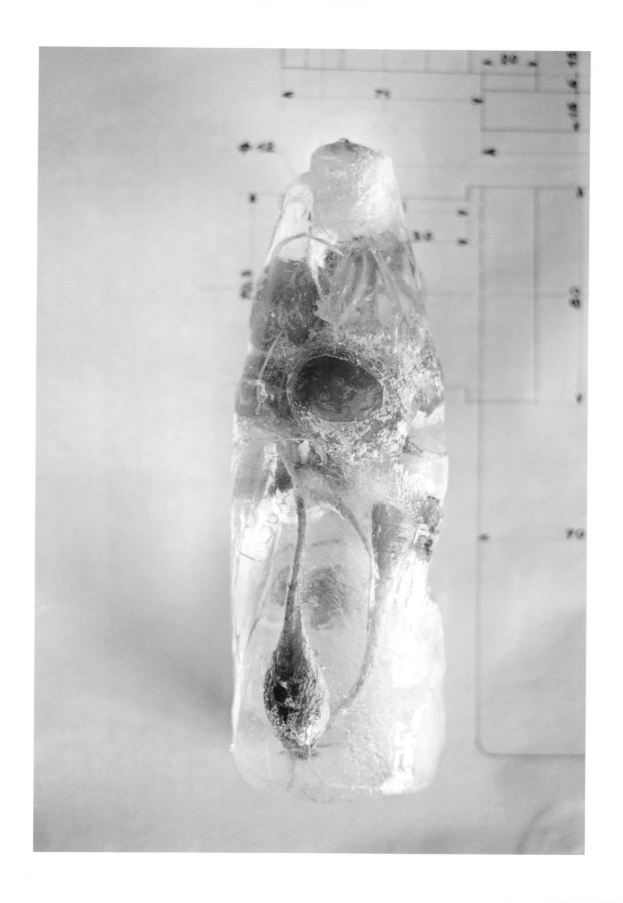

195

# POT OF PEAS

FOR 4

620 g (1 lb 6 oz/4 cups) fresh shelled peas
80 ml (2½ fl oz/⅓ cup) lemon juice
80 ml (2½ fl oz/⅓ cup) extra virgin olive oil
1 tablespoon pink lake salt
80 ml (2½ fl oz/⅓ cup) creamy dressing (page 124)
120 g (4¼ oz/2 cups) pea shoots

Place the shelled peas in a sealed plastic bag in the freezer for 10 hours.

Put the peas in a large bowl and pour over enough boiling water to cover. Place a chopping board over the bowl for 1 minute.

Drain the peas and return to the bowl. Add the lemon juice, olive oil and salt, and mix well.

Divide the peas between four bowls and top each with a quarter of the creamy dressing and the pea shoots.

# AVOCADO, TUSCAN KALE, PESTO AND CLASSIC CHEESE SALAD

FOR 4

2 avocados, spooned into chunks
1 small bunch of baby Tuscan kale (black kale), roughly torn
210 g (7½ oz/1 cup) basil and kale pesto (page 113)
100 g (3½ oz/½ cup) classic cashew cheese (page 80)


Put all the ingredients in a large bowl and gently combine them with your hands.

Divide the salad between four bowls and serve immediately.

# CHOP CHOP SALAD

FOR 4

3 cucumbers, diced
4 tomatoes, diced
1 red capsicum (pepper), diced
1 celery stalk, diced
½ cup dehydrated olives (page 58)
60 ml (2 fl oz/¼ cup) citrus dressing (page 121)

Put all the ingredients in a large bowl and combine gently with your hands.

Divide the salad between four bowls to serve.

NOTE You could add some freshly grated ginger to this salad.

# CAESAR SALAD WITH CRUSHED WALNUTS

FOR 4

200 g (7 oz/1 cup) walnut cashew cheese (page 82)
250 ml (9 fl oz/1 cup) extra virgin olive oil
juice of 2 limes
4 baby cos (romaine) lettuces, shredded
70 g (2½ oz/½ cup) walnut pieces, roughly crushed

Put the walnut cashew cheese in a blender with the olive oil and lime juice, and blend for 30 seconds.

Put the shredded lettuce in a large bowl with the cheese mix and the walnuts.

Gently mix, then divide between four plates and serve immediately.

# BABY SPINACH, CORIANDER, CUCUMBER AND GINGER SALAD

FOR 4

3 large handfuls baby English spinach leaves
1 large handful coriander (cilantro) leaves
4 cucumbers, sliced
2 teaspoons freshly grated ginger
125 ml (4 fl oz/½ cup) miso dressing (page 123)

Using your hands, gently combine all the ingredients in a large bowl.

Divide the salad between four bowls to serve.

# SHREDDED LETTUCE AND SPEARMINT WITH LEMON-LIME DRESSING

FOR 4

1 small iceberg lettuce, shredded
1 small handful spearmint leaves
juice of 2 lemons
juice of 2 limes
60 ml (2 fl oz/¼ cup) extra virgin olive oil
½ teaspoon pink lake salt


Using your hands, combine all the ingredients in a large bowl.

Divide the salad between four bowls to serve.

# BEETROOT, GINGER AND MIXED HERB SALAD

FOR 4

280 g (10 oz/2 cups) freshly grated beetroot (beets)
2 teaspoons freshly grated ginger
1 handful flat-leaf (Italian) parsley leaves
1 handful mint leaves
1 handful coriander (cilantro) leaves
125 ml (4 fl oz/½ cup) sesame dressing (page 122)

Using your hands, gently combine all the ingredients in a large bowl.

Divide the salad between four bowls to serve.

more raw

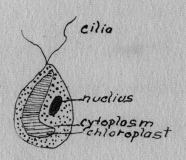

cilia

nuclius

cytoplasm
chloroplast

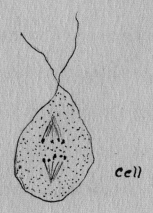

Cell

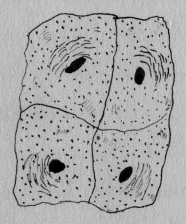

Reproduction

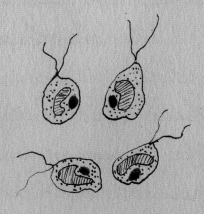

4 new plants

# SPICY TOMATO 'LINGUINE'

FOR 4

300 g (10½ oz) butternut pumpkin (squash)
80 ml (2½ fl oz/⅓ cup) extra virgin olive oil
½ teaspoon pink lake salt
205 g (7¼ oz/1 cup) spicy tomato relish (page 117)
65 g (2¼ oz/⅓ cup) lemon and dill cashew cheese (page 81)
1 small handful basil leaves

Using a large potato peeler, slice the butternut pumpkin into paper-thin slices lengthwise. They should be the width of linguine.

Combine the pumpkin 'linguine' in a large bowl with the oil and salt, and set aside for 5 minutes.

Divide the 'linguine' between four bowls and top each with a quarter of the tomato relish, lemon and dill cashew cheese and basil.

# CAPSICUMS WITH LEMON, GARLIC AND LEMON AND DILL CHEESE

FOR 4

2 lemons, cut into thin wedges
1 small handful coriander (cilantro) leaves, torn
1 small handful flat-leaf (Italian) parsley, torn
80 ml (2½ fl oz/⅓ cup) extra virgin olive oil
2 teaspoons tamari
2 teaspoons freshly ground black pepper
2 dehydrated red capsicums (peppers) (page 60)
2 dehydrated green capsicums (peppers) (page 60)
8 dehydrated garlic cloves (page 62)
65 g (2¼ oz/⅓ cup) lemon and dill cashew cheese (page 81) (optional)

Put the lemon wedges in the freezer overnight, or until frozen.

Mix the torn coriander and parsley leaves in a large bowl with the olive oil, tamari, black pepper and lemon wedges.

Pour the lemon mixture onto a baking tray lined with baking paper and place the tray in the dehydrator for 1 hour.

Divide the mixture between four bowls and top with the capsicums, garlic and lemon and dill cashew cheese (if using).

# POT PIE

FOR 4

125 g (4½ oz/½ cup) cashew mayonnaise (page 77)
¼ cup dehydrated red onions (page 58)
¼ cup dehydrated mushrooms (page 55)
¼ cup dehydrated olives (page 58)
¼ cup dehydrated tomatoes (page 57)
¼ cup dehydrated garlic cloves (page 62), skins removed
2 orange thyme sprigs
2 x savoury tart bases (page 105)

In a large bowl, gently combine the mayonnaise, onions, mushrooms, olives, tomatoes, garlic and thyme.

Crumble the tart bases. Divide the vegetable mixture between four small pots or bowls and top each one with tart crumble.

Put the small pot pies in the dehydrator for 1 hour.

Remove from the dehydrator and serve with your favourite salad from the salad section (pages 184-207).

ALTERNATIVE If you can't get your hands on orange thyme, either lemon thyme or regular thyme would be a good substitute.

# NETTLE PESTO BISCUITS WITH DEHYDRATED TOMATOES

FOR 4

400 g (14 oz/2 cups) classic cashew cheese (page 80)
80 g (2¾ oz/⅓ cup) nettle pesto (page 114)
4 dehydrated tomatoes (page 57)

Place four 8 cm (3¼ in) pastry rings on a baking tray lined with baking paper.

Gently combine the cheese and pesto in a medium bowl.

Divide the cheese mixture between the rings, spreading to flatten, and place the tray in the dehydrator for 8 hours.

Place on a wire cooling rack for 5 minutes and then serve topped with the tomato.

# BASIL AND KALE PESTO 'FETTUCCINE'

FOR 4

4 zucchini (courgettes), about 65 g (2¼ oz)
80 ml (2½ fl oz/⅓ cup) extra virgin olive oil
½ teaspoon pink lake salt
210 g (7½ oz/1 cup) basil and kale pesto (page 113)
65 g (2¼ oz/⅓ cup) classic cashew cheese (page 80)
1 small handful basil leaves

Peel the zucchini and slice them paper-thin lengthwise with a large potato peeler. Combine with the olive oil and salt in a large bowl and set aside for 5 minutes.

Divide the zucchini 'fettucine' between four bowls and top each with a quarter of the pesto, classic cashew cheese and basil.

# SWISS BROWN MUSHROOM, MICRO BASIL AND PEA 'RISOTTO'

FOR 4

½ cauliflower, broken into florets
75 g (2½ oz/½ cup) frozen peas
1 cup dehydrated Swiss brown mushrooms (page 55)
65 g (2¼ oz/⅓ cup) classic cashew cheese (page 80)
80 ml (2½ fl oz/⅓ cup) extra virgin olive oil
1 tablespoon tamari
½ teaspoon freshly ground black pepper
1 small handful micro basil or small basil leaves

Process the cauliflower florets in a food processor for 4 seconds.

Rinse the peas under warm running water in a colander for 1 minute.

Gently combine the cauliflower, peas, mushrooms, cashew cheese, olive oil, tamari and pepper in a large bowl.

Divide the risotto between four bowls and scatter over the basil leaves.

# WALNUT BOLOGNESE 'SPAGHETTI'

FOR 4

4 zucchini (courgettes), peeled
80 ml (2½ fl oz/⅓ cup) extra virgin olive oil
½ teaspoon pink lake salt
200 g (7 oz/1 cup) walnut bolognese (page 116)
1 small handful basil leaves

Cut the zucchini into fine strips with a julienne peeler. Combine with the olive oil and salt in a large bowl and set aside for 5 minutes.

Divide the zucchini 'spaghetti' into four bowls and top each bowl with a quarter of the walnut bolognese and the basil leaves.


# GLAZED HEIRLOOM BABY CARROTS

FOR 4

12 dehydrated baby heirloom carrots (page 54)
80 g (2¾ oz/⅓ cup) vanilla cashew cream (page 74)
2 tablespoons horseradish dressing (page 122)
¼ cup micro carrot tops (optional)

Divide the carrots between four plates and top each with a quarter of the vanilla cashew cream, horseradish dressing and micro carrot tops (if using).

NOTE The micro carrot tops bring a lovely licorice flavour to the dish.

# DEHYDRATED ONION WITH THYME, BASIL AND WALNUT CHEESE

FOR 4

6 dehydrated red onions (page 58), but cut the onions in half and combine with
    6 orange thyme (or lemon thyme) sprigs when preparing them
2 large handfuls micro basil or baby rocket
65 g (2¼ oz/⅓ cup) walnut cashew cheese (page 82)

Serve the onions with the rocket and walnut cashew cheese.

NOTE Serve everything individually on a platter, or gently combine in a large bowl as a salad.

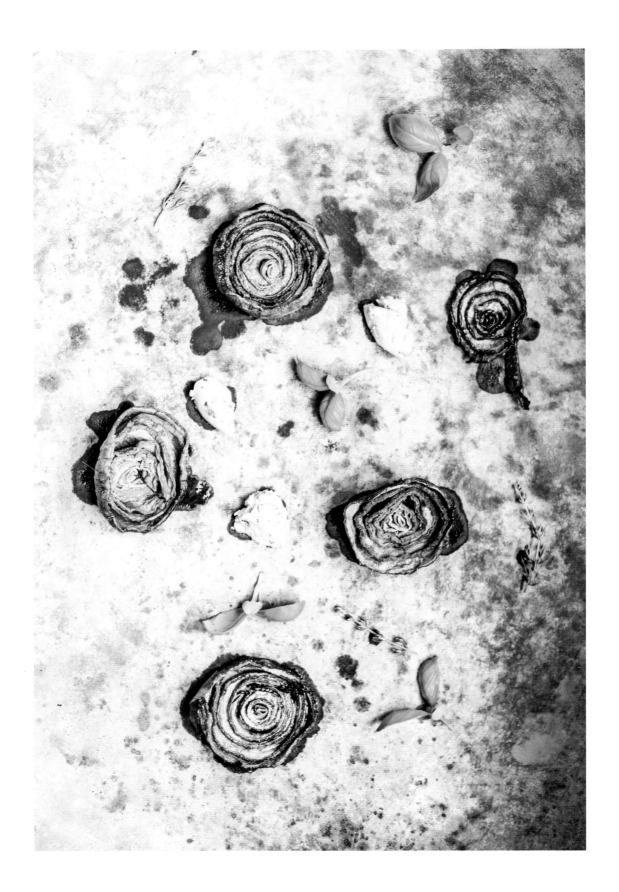

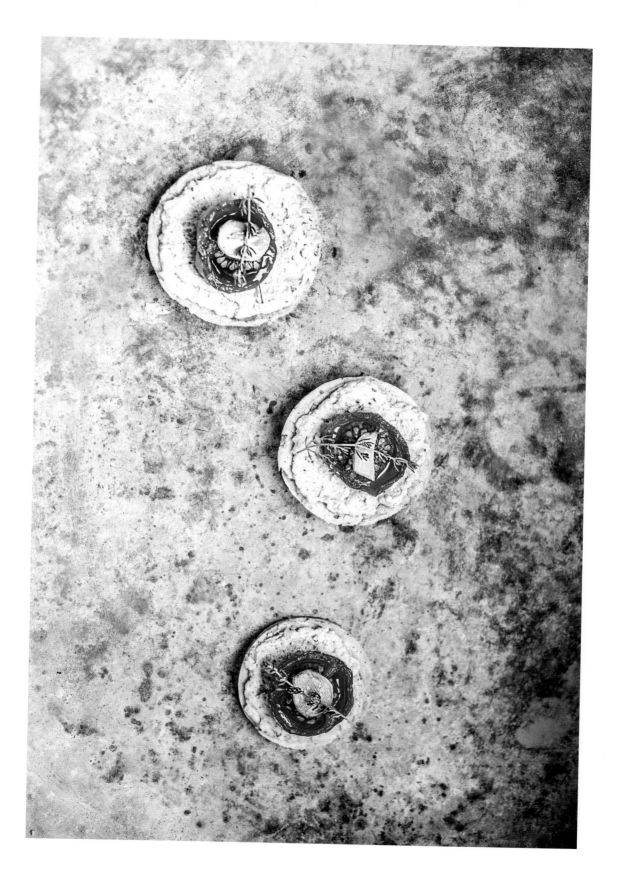

GLAZED HEIRLOOM BABY CARROTS

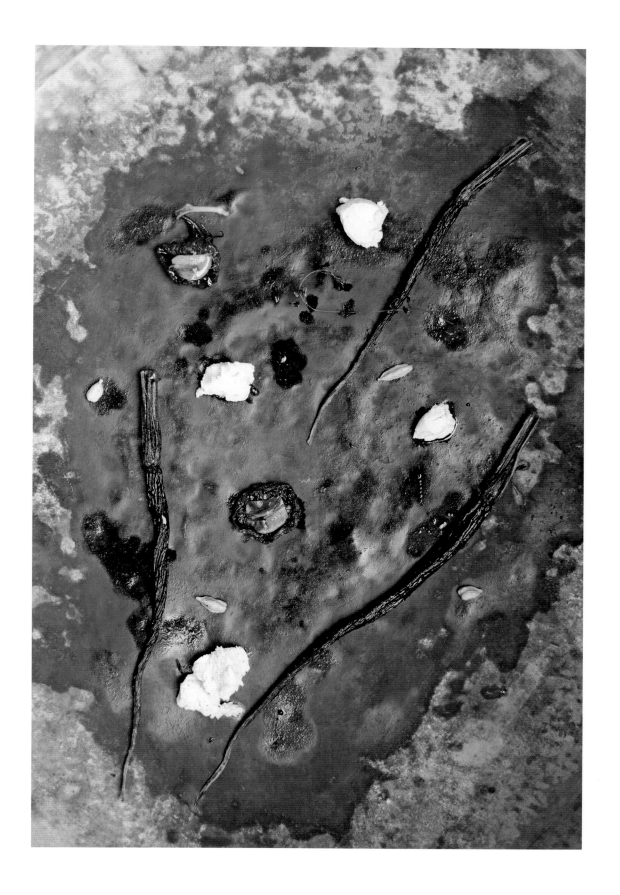

# BROAD BEAN, DEHYDRATED GARLIC AND ASPARAGUS 'RISOTTO'

FOR 4

½ cauliflower, broken into florets
80 g (2¾ oz/½ cup) frozen broad beans
1 cup dehydrated asparagus (follow method for dehydrated fennel bulbs, page 56), sliced
4 dehydrated garlic cloves (page 62), skins removed and flesh thinly sliced
65 g (2¼ oz/⅓ cup) lemon and dill cashew cheese (page 81)
80 ml (2½ fl oz/⅓ cup) extra virgin olive oil
1 tablespoon tamari
½ teaspoon freshly ground black pepper
1 small handful micro mint or small mint leaves

Process the cauliflower florets in a food processor for 4 seconds.

Rinse the broad beans under warm running water in a colander for 1 minute, then peel them.

Gently combine the cauliflower, broad beans, asparagus, garlic, lemon and dill cashew cheese, olive oil, tamari and pepper in a large bowl.

Divide the risotto between four bowls and sprinkle with the mint leaves.

# dessert

Female Plant.

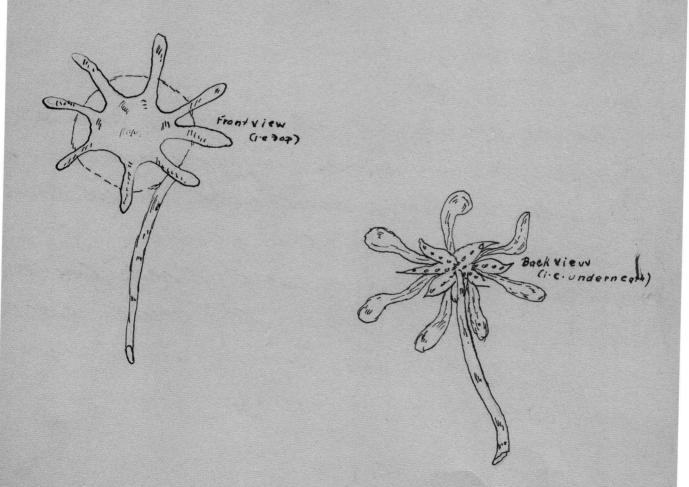

Front view
(i.e Top)

Back view
(i.e. underneath)

ROSEWATER GRANITA WITH MICRO SHISO

# ROSEWATER GRANITA WITH MICRO SHISO

FOR 8

1 litre (35 fl oz/4 cups) water
80 ml (2½ fl oz/⅓ cup) rosewater
½ teaspoon guar gum
½ cardamom pod, seeds only
5 g (⅛ oz/½ cup) micro shiso

Blend the water, rosewater, guar gum and cardamom in a blender for 1 minute.

Pour into a deep baking tray and freeze for 10 hours.

Using a fork, scrape into a medium bowl and return to the freezer for 10 minutes.

Serve the granita in individual bowls, glasses or cups and scatter with the micro shiso.

NOTE The sweetness of the rosewater and the short-lived sweet-sour taste of the micro shiso are a great match. The micro shiso is very refreshing, a wonderful palate cleanser in summer.

ALTERNATIVE If you don't have micro shiso at hand, substitute with your choice of herb, such as mint, basil or lemon thyme.

# BLUEBERRY PORT GEL WITH GRANITA

FOR 8

620 g (1 lb 6 oz/4 cups) blueberries
1 litre (35 fl oz/4 cups) port
2 teaspoons guar gum
500 ml (17 fl oz/2 cups) water
2 cardamom pods, seeds only

To prepare the blueberry gel, put the blueberries on a baking tray lined with baking paper and place it in the dehydrator for 4 hours.

Mix the blueberries and port in a large bowl and set aside for 2 hours.

Blend the port, blueberries and 1 ½ teaspoons guar gum in a blender for 1 minute.

Pour the blueberry mixture into a container, and refrigerate for 10 hours.

To prepare the granita, blend the water, ½ teaspoon of guar gum and the cardamom seeds in the blender for 1 minute.

Pour into a deep baking tray and freeze for 10 hours.

Using a fork, scrape the mixture into a medium bowl and return to the freezer for 10 minutes.

Serve the granita and blueberry gel together in individual bowls, glasses or cups.

# WHITE CHOCOLATE AND MANGO SORBET

FOR 4

800 g (1 lb 12 oz) mango flesh, about 3 mangoes
250 ml (9 fl oz/1 cup) young Thai coconut water
2 tablespoons cacao butter, melted

Blend all the ingredients in a blender for 1 minute.

Pour into your choice of sorbet maker/ice-cream maker, and churn according to the manufacturer's instructions.

Alternatively, line a square container with plastic wrap and pour in the blended mixture. Freeze overnight.

If freezing overnight, pop out the frozen block the following day. Chop into large pieces and put into the food processor. Pulse until the sorbet has the desired consistency (lovely, smooth and creamy).

Serve in individual bowls, glasses or cups.

# VICTORIAN NAVEL ORANGE SORBET

FOR 4

500 ml (17 fl oz/2 cups) navel orange juice
4 large apricots, peeled and stones removed
125 ml (4 fl oz/½ cup) coconut nectar
½ teaspoon vanilla bean paste (page 118)
½ teaspoon vanilla salt (page 103)

Blend all the ingredients in a blender for 2 minutes.

Pour into your choice of sorbet maker/ice-cream maker, and churn according to the manufacturer's instructions.

Alternatively, line a square container with plastic wrap and pour in the blended mixture. Freeze overnight.

If freezing overnight, pop out the frozen block the following day. Chop into large pieces and put into the food processor. Pulse until the sorbet has the desired consistency (lovely, smooth and creamy).

Serve in individual bowls, glasses or cups.

NOTE I like to call this dish Victorian navel orange sorbet because I always source my fresh produce locally. We can all try and do our bit to help local farmers.

235

# ALMOND COINTREAU ICE-CREAM

MAKES 650 G (1 LB 7 OZ)

80 g (2¾ oz/½ cup) raw almonds
125 ml (4 fl oz/½ cup) coconut nectar
155 g (5½ oz/1 cup) cashews
250 ml (9 fl oz/1 cup) water
60 ml (2 fl oz/¼ cup) Cointreau or other orange-flavoured liqueur
2 teaspoons vanilla bean paste (page 118)
¼ teaspoon vanilla salt (page 103)
125 ml (4 fl oz/½ cup) coconut oil, melted
2 teaspoons cacao butter, melted

Combine the almonds and half the coconut nectar in a small bowl.

Spread the coated almonds on a baking tray lined with baking paper. Put in the dehydrator for 4 hours.

Remove the baking tray from the dehydrator and put in the freezer for 1 hour.

Pulse the almonds in a food processor for 2 seconds until the mix has a lovely praline texture.

Blend the cashews and water in a blender until smooth.

Add the remaining half of the coconut nectar to the cashew mix, along with the Cointreau, vanilla bean paste and vanilla salt, and blend for a further 10 seconds.

Add the coconut oil and cacao butter and blend for a further 5 seconds until combined.

Add the almond mixture and combine for a further 2 seconds.

Churn in an ice-cream machine according to the manufacturer's instructions, or pour into a container, cover and put in the freezer for about 12 hours or until frozen.

# WHITE PEACH AND BLOOD ORANGE GRANITA

FOR 8

4 large white peaches, peeled and stones removed
500 ml (17 fl oz/2 cups) blood orange juice
½ teaspoon vanilla bean paste (page 118)
½ teaspoon vanilla salt (page 103)


Blend all the ingredients in a blender for 1 minute.

Pour into a deep baking tray and freeze for 10 hours.

Using a fork, scrape the mixture into a medium bowl and return to the freezer for 10 minutes.

Serve in individual bowls, glasses or cups.

# SALTED CARAMEL WITH DEHYDRATED ALMOND PUDDING

FOR 4

160 g (5¾ oz/1 cup) raw almonds
480 g (1 lb 1 oz/2 cups) cashew mascarpone (page 84)
235 g (8½ oz/1 cup) salted caramel (page 120)
55 g (2 oz) biscuits (page 106)
35 g (1¼ oz/¼ cup) cacao nibs

Spread the almonds on a baking tray lined with baking paper. Put the tray in the dehydrator for 4 hours.

Gently crush the almonds.

Layer all the ingredients in four glass jars or dishes and refrigerate for 2 hours to enable the flavours to develop.

# COCONUT SEMIFREDDO WITH FIG JAM
# AND CRUSHED PISTACHIO NUTS

FOR 4

480 g (1 lb 1 oz/2 cups) coconut semifreddo (opposite)
320 g (11¼ oz/1 cup) fig jam (page 95)
70 g (2½ oz/½ cup) pistachio kernels, crushed
35 g (1¼ oz/¼ cup) cacao nibs
1 small handful micro mint

Layer all the ingredients in four glass jars or dishes, and refrigerate for 2 hours to enable the flavours to develop.

NOTE The mint breaks through the richness of the dessert and adds a refreshing aftertone.

# SPOTTED DICK PUDDING

FOR 4

700 g (1 lb 9 oz/3 cups) salted caramel (page 120)
55 g (2 oz) biscuits (page 106)
85 g (3 oz) raisins, currants or sultanas (golden raisins)
160 g (5½ oz/½ cup) saffron orange marmalade (page 97)

Layer all the ingredients in four glass jars or dishes and refrigerate for 2 hours to enable the flavours to develop.


# COCONUT SEMIFREDDO

FOR 8

500 ml (17 fl oz/2 cups) young Thai coconut water
150 g (5½ oz) young Thai coconut meat
155 g (5½ oz/1 cup) cashews
125 ml (4 fl oz/½ cup) coconut nectar
2 tablespoons rum
2 teaspoons vanilla bean paste (page 118)
¼ teaspoon vanilla salt (page 103)
250 ml (9 fl oz/1 cup) coconut oil, melted

Blend the coconut water, coconut meat and cashews in a blender until smooth.

Add the coconut nectar, rum, vanilla bean paste and vanilla salt, and blend for a further 10 seconds. Add the coconut oil and blend for a further 5 seconds.

Put in a container and freeze for 12 hours to set.

Serve in individual bowls, glasses or cups.

NOTE This delicious semifreddo is particularly good paired with jams.

# MELBOURNE NIGHTS

FOR 4

520 g (1 lb 2½ oz/2 cups) chocolate mousse (page 260)
55 g (2 oz) biscuits (page 106), crushed
360 g (12¾ oz/1½ cups) cashew mascarpone (page 84)
35 g (1¼ oz/¼ cup) cacao nibs

Layer all the ingredients in four glass jars or dishes and refrigerate for 2 hours to enable the flavours to develop.

NOTE Sprinkle with shavings of raw vegan chocolate if desired.

# MINT SLICE ICE-CREAM

MAKES 600 G (1 LB 5 OZ)

155 g (5½ oz/1 cup) cashews
250 ml (9 fl oz/1 cup) water
60 ml (2 fl oz/¼ cup) coconut nectar
2 tablespoons rum
½ teaspoon mint essence
2 teaspoons vanilla bean paste (page 118)
½ teaspoon vanilla salt (page 103)
125 ml (4 fl oz/½ cup) coconut oil, melted
2 teaspoons cacao butter, melted
35 g (1¼ oz/¼ cup) cacao nibs

Blend the cashews and water in a blender until smooth.

Add the coconut nectar, rum, mint essence, vanilla bean paste and vanilla salt, and blend for a further 10 seconds.

Add the coconut oil, cacao butter and cacao nibs, and blend for a further 2 seconds until combined.

Churn in an ice-cream machine according to the manufacturer's instructions, or pour into a container, cover and put in the freezer for about 12 hours or until frozen.

# STICKY DATE PUDDING

FOR 4

480 g (1 lb 1 oz/2 cups) cashew mascarpone (page 84)
350 g (12 oz/1½ cups) salted caramel (page 120)
55 g (2 oz) biscuits (page 106), crushed
35 g (1¼ oz/¼ cup) cacao nibs

Layer all the ingredients in four glass jars or dishes and refrigerate for 2 hours to enable the flavours to develop.

NOTE Sprinkle with shavings of raw vegan chocolate if desired.

# TIRAMISU-ISH

FOR 4

480 g (1 lb 1 oz/2 cups) cashew mascarpone (page 84)
55 g (2 oz) biscuits (page 106), crushed
250 ml (9 fl oz/1 cup) coffee syrup (page 120)
35 g (1¼ oz/¼ cup) cacao nibs

Layer all the ingredients in four glass jars or dishes and refrigerate for 2 hours to enable the flavours to develop.

NOTE This delicious light dessert gives you all the flavour experience of the traditional tiramisu without the bloated after-effects.

ALTERNATIVE If you don't have the coffee syrup at hand, you can replace with cooled, freshly brewed coffee. However, you will lose a level of depth and richness.

chocolate

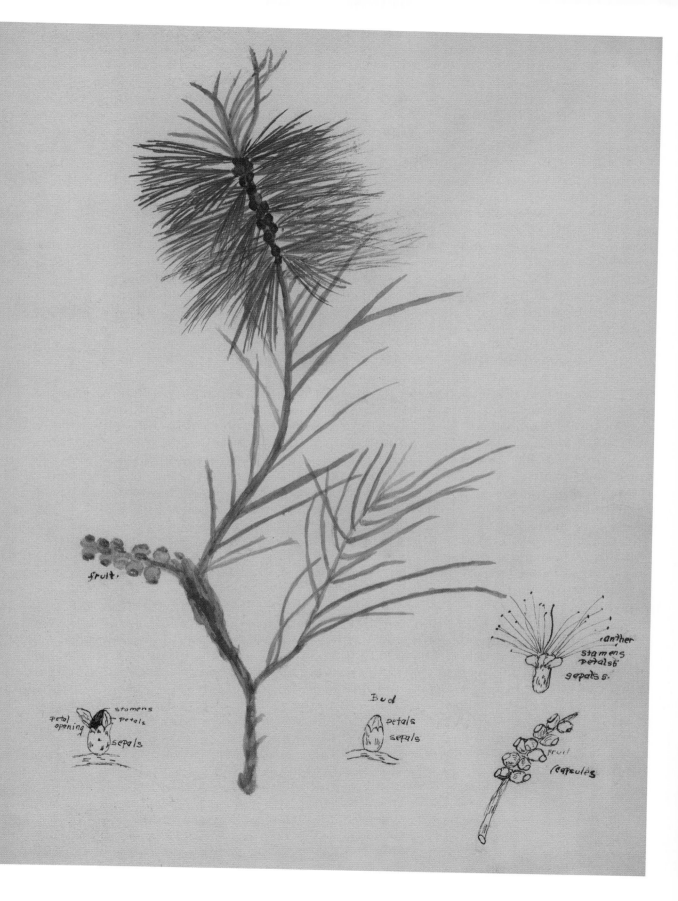

fruit.

stamens
Petal Petals
opening sepals

Bud
petals
sepals

anther
stamens
petals 6
sepals 5.

fruit
capsules

# TEMPERED CHOCOLATE

MAKES 875 G (1 LB 15 OZ)

575 g (1 lb 4½ oz/2½ cups) cacao butter
1 tablespoon vanilla bean paste (page 118)
½ teaspoon vanilla salt (page 103)
200 g (7 oz/2 cups) cacao powder, sifted
125 ml (4 fl oz/½ cup) coconut nectar

Finely chop the cacao butter and place in a metal bowl. Put the bowl over a medium saucepan of water over low heat. Melt the butter slowly, stirring constantly with a silicone spatula until just melted, taking care not to heat above 43°C (110°F).

Stir in the vanilla bean paste and vanilla salt,

Add the cacao powder, 50 g (1¾ oz/½ cup) at a time, mixing well after each addition and ensuring there are no lumps.

Place the coconut nectar in a metal bowl. Put the bowl over a medium saucepan of water over low heat. Warm slowly, stirring constantly with a silicone spatula, for 10 minutes, or until it just reaches 43°C (110°F).

Slowly add the coconut nectar to the cacao butter mixture, stirring to combine. It is essential that you do not add the coconut nectar too quickly or the temperature will drop too fast.

Use the liquid chocolate for dipping or put aside to set.

NOTE The chocolate mixture needs to be a target temperature of approximately 41–43°C (105–110°F). You do not want it to go above this temperature or the chocolate will scorch. Once the mixture has melted, remove the bowl from the heat. Be careful that no steam from the water gets into the chocolate. Continue to stir the chocolate until it has cooled to approximately 29°C (85°F). Place a cool, dry knife in the chocolate to test if the mixture has tempered. It should begin to harden quickly.

NOTE If you're planning to use the chocolate for dipping, you've got about 15 minutes before it starts to set. If your preference is delicious, hard chocolate, pour the liquid into a mould of your choice, simply plain or mixed through with your favourite dried fruits or food-grade essences.

NOTE If you do not warm the coconut nectar, the chocolate may bloom (becoming dusty or mottled in appearance).

# FRENCH VANILLA ICE-CREAM DIPPED IN BITTER CHOCOLATE

FOR 8

600 g (1 lb 5 oz/4 cups) French vanilla ice-cream (page 85)
8 licorice sticks
liquid tempered chocolate (page 252), or purchase raw vegan chocolate and melt
extra tempered chocolate, set and shaved, to serve

Divide the ice-cream between eight espresso glasses and freeze for 2 hours.

Remove from the freezer and place a licorice stick in the centre of each. Return to the freezer for 10 hours.

Separate the ice-cream from the sides of the glasses with a small thin-bladed knife and gently pull on the licorice stick to remove the ice-cream from the glasses. Dip the ice-creams into the melted chocolate to coat and sprinkle with the shaved chocolate.

Place the ice-creams on a baking tray lined with baking paper and return to the freezer for 10 minutes to set.

# WAGON WHEELS

FOR 8

125 g (4½ oz) vanilla cashew cream (page 74)
60 g (2¼ oz) agent six praline (page 119)
biscuits (page 106), made using 6 cm (2½ in) rings
500 ml (17 fl oz/2 cups) liquid tempered chocolate (page 252)

Place the vanilla cashew cream and praline in a blender and blend for 5 seconds to combine.

Put the mixture into a small bowl and place in the freezer for 20 minutes.

Spread the mixture on half of the biscuits and place the other biscuits on top.

Put the biscuits on a baking tray lined with baking paper and put in the freezer for 1 hour.

Pour the liquid tempered chocolate into a bowl. Dip the biscuits into the chocolate, coating well, and place on the baking tray. Return to the freezer for another 10 minutes.

Store in a sterilised glass jar in a dry cool place. These will keep for up to 1 week.


# CHOCOLATE DRINK

MAKES 500 G (1 LB 2 OZ)

500 g (1 lb 2 oz) cacao (chocolate) liquor, melted
1 tablespoon vanilla bean paste (page 118)
½ teaspoon vanilla salt (page 103)
70 g (2½ oz/½ cup) coconut sugar

Pour the cacao liquor into a medium bowl, add the vanilla bean paste and vanilla salt and whisk to combine.

Pour the mixture into a shallow baking tray lined with baking paper. Set aside for a minute before evenly sprinkling the coconut sugar on top.

Place in the refrigerator for 1 hour to set. Once set, break it into pieces and store in a sterilised glass jar in a cool dry place for up to 1 month.

To serve, simply mix the desired amount with hot water.

# CHOCOLATE SORBET

MAKES 1 KG (2 LB 4 OZ)

155 g (5½ oz/1 cup) cashews
500 ml (17 fl oz/2 cups) water
250 ml (9 fl oz/1 cup) coconut nectar
1 tablespoon vanilla bean paste (page 118)
½ teaspoon vanilla salt (page 103)
1 teaspoon carob bean gum
150 g (5½ oz/1½ cups) cacao powder

Put the cashews and water in a blender and blend for 1 minute.

Add the coconut nectar, vanilla bean paste, vanilla salt and carob bean gum. Blend for 10 seconds.

Sift the cacao powder into the mixture and blend on low for 1 minute or until combined.

Churn in an ice-cream machine according to the manufacturer's instructions, or pour into a metal container, cover and put in the freezer for about 12 hours or until frozen.

NOTE You can sprinkle cacao nibs on top before it sets, if you like.

# CHOCOLATE MOUSSE

MAKES 875 G (1 LB 15 OZ)

450 g (1 lb) diced mango flesh, about 2 small mangoes
250 ml (9 fl oz/1 cup) coconut nectar
1 tablespoon vanilla bean paste (page 118)
½ teaspoon vanilla salt (page 103)
2 tablespoons coconut oil, melted
2 tablespoons cacao butter, melted
200 g (7 oz/2 cups) cacao powder

Put the mango, coconut nectar, vanilla bean paste and vanilla salt in a blender and blend for 1 minute before adding the coconut oil and cacao butter. Pulse to combine.

Sift the cacao powder into the blender. Blend on low for 1 minute to combine.

Pour into a container and refrigerate for 10 hours. Alternatively, pour into several small bowls to serve as individual desserts.

This will keep in the refrigerator for up to 1 week.

# CHOCOLATE MOUSSE WITH CHOCOLATE SOIL

FOR 4

60 g (2¼ oz/½ cup) chocolate soil (page 108)
85 g (3 oz/⅓ cup) chocolate mousse (above)
vanilla salt (page 103), to serve (optional)

Sprinkle a quarter of the chocolate soil on each of four plates and top each with a quarter of the chocolate mousse. Sprinkle with vanilla salt (if using).

# CHOCOLATE FUDGE

MAKES 725 G (1 LB 10 OZ)

250 ml (9 fl oz/1 cup) coconut nectar
155 g (5½ oz/1 cup) cashews
1 tablespoon vanilla bean paste (page 118)
½ teaspoon vanilla salt (page 103)
230 g (8 oz/1 cup) cacao butter, melted
100 g (3½ oz/1 cup) cacao powder

Put the coconut nectar, cashews, vanilla bean paste and vanilla salt in a blender and blend for 1 minute.

Add the cacao butter and blend for 10 seconds.

Sift the cacao powder onto the mixture and blend on low for 10 seconds until combined.

Pour onto a baking tray lined with baking paper, cover with another layer of baking paper, and store in a cool dry place for up to 1 week. Cut into squares to serve.

NOTE You can sprinkle chocolate soil (page 108) or crushed pistachios on top before it sets.

# AGENT SIX CHOCOLATE FUDGE

MAKES 345 G (12 OZ)

120 g (4¼ oz/½ cup) agent six praline (page 119)
190 g (6¾ oz/½ cup) chocolate fudge (see above)
35 g (1¼ oz/¼ cup) cacao nibs

Layer all the ingredients in four sterilised glass jars or dishes and refrigerate for 2 hours to enable the flavours to develop.

AGENT SIX CHOCOLATE FUDGE

# CHOCOLATE CRUMBLE, MARMALADE AND VANILLA CREAM

FOR 4

4 tablespoons cacao beans
80 ml (2½ fl oz/⅓ cup) rosewater
2 x sweet tart bases (page 105), made with 1 tablespoon cacao powder added
115 g (4 oz/⅓ cup) saffron orange marmalade (page 97)
80 g (2¾ oz) vanilla cashew cream (page 74)

Combine the cacao beans and rosewater in a small bowl.

Spread the coated cacao beans on a baking tray lined with baking paper and place in the dehydrator for 4 hours.

Gently crush the beans.

Crumble the tart bases and divide between four sterilised glass jars. Top with the marmalade, vanilla cashew cream and crushed cacao beans. Refrigerate for 2 hours to enable the flavours to develop.


# LUCUMA CHOCOLATE CRUMBLE WITH VANILLA PEACH JAM PUDDING

FOR 4

2 x sweet tart bases (page 105), made with 1 tablespoon lucuma powder added
125 g (4½ oz) cacao (chocolate) liquor, melted
115 g (4 oz/⅓ cup) vanilla peach jam (page 93)
80 g (2¾ oz) vanilla cashew cream (page 74)

Crumble the tart bases and divide between four sterilised glass jars or dishes. Top with the cacao liquor, jam and cream. Refrigerate for 2 hours to enable the flavours to develop.

# CHOCOLATE ICE-CREAM

MAKES 710 G (1 LB 9 OZ)

155 g (5½ oz/1 cup) cashews
250 ml (9 fl oz/1 cup) water
125 ml (4 fl oz/½ cup) coconut nectar
2 tablespoons port
1 tablespoon freshly brewed coffee
2 teaspoons vanilla bean paste (page 118)
¼ teaspoon vanilla salt (page 103)
1 teaspoon lecithin
1 teaspoon guar gum
1 teaspoon carob bean gum
100 g (3½ oz/1 cup) cacao powder

Put the cashews and water in a blender and blend until smooth.

Add the coconut nectar, port, coffee, vanilla bean paste and vanilla salt, and blend for 10 seconds.

Add the lecithin, guar gum and carob bean gum and pulse to combine.

Sift the cacao powder into the blender and blend on low for 1 minute until combined.

Churn in an ice-cream machine according to the manufacturer's instructions, or pour into a metal container, cover and put in the freezer for about 12 hours or until frozen.

# COFFEE-INFUSED 'HOT CHOCOLATE' WITH HAZELNUT FROTH

FOR 4

1 litre (35 fl oz/4 cups) cashew milk (page 74)
250 g (9 oz/1 cup) chocolate drink (page 257)
60 ml ( 2 fl oz/¼ cup) chocolate and coffee agave syrup (page 108)
75 g (2½ oz/½ cup) hazelnuts
250 ml (9 fl oz/1 cup) water

Blend the cashew milk, chocolate drink and chocolate and coffee agave syrup in a blender for 5 minutes. Pour into four cups.

Blend the hazelnuts and water in a blender for 2 minutes. Spoon the frothy part of the hazelnut mixture over the chocolate in the cups. Serve immediately.


# PEPPERMINT CHOCOLATE

MAKES 300 G (10½ OZ)

500 ml (17 fl oz/2 cups) liquid tempered chocolate (page 252)
½ teaspoon peppermint essence

Combine the liquid tempered chocolate and mint essence, then pour into a silicone mould or moulds of your choice.

Refrigerate for 2 hours or until set.

# RASPBERRY SOUP WITH CHOCOLATE SORBET

FOR 4

5 lemon thyme sprigs
250 g (9 oz/2 cups) frozen raspberries
125 ml (4 fl oz/½ cup) sparkling mineral water
2 tablespoons lime juice
2 tablespoons vanilla bean paste (page 118)
75 g (2½ oz/½ cup) chocolate sorbet (page 258), to serve

Pick the leaves from the lemon thyme and put in a blender with the raspberries, sparkling mineral water, lime juice and vanilla bean paste. Blend for 3 minutes.

Divide the raspberry mixture between four bowls and top with the chocolate sorbet.

index

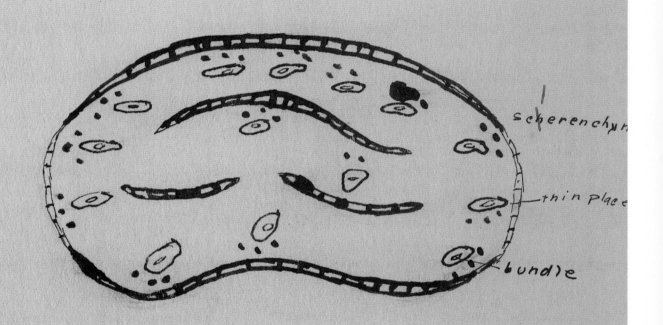

scherenchyn

thin place

bundle

acknowledgments

The botanical illustrations in this book were created by Kathleen Helena Halley Lowery (née Longhurst) - my grandmother, known to me as Kath.

Kathleen was born in the Victorian goldfields town of Clunes in 1910. Her father, Josiah, was a mining engineer whose job was to maintain stationary factory engines. Kath moved to Sydney with her mother, Alice, and three siblings after her father's sudden death in a workplace accident.

In her final year at St George Girls' High, in 1927, Kath was awarded first place in Art. At teachers' college she was able to join Botany classes with university degree students.

In 1930 Kath officially entered the New South Wales teaching service. Teaching was one of the strong threads of her life, something she always came back to until her retirement in the early 1980s.

While sorting through my grandmother's belongings a decade after her death, I came across her senior school exercise books. Opening the brown paper-covered botany books fills me with joy and admiration for Kath's early artworks. Facing each page of handwritten notes is a pen or watercolour illustration of the plant and its parts.

I always admired Kath's artistic talent and dedication to education - and I adored her cooking. There are many precious memories tied up with image, flavours, fragrance and, of course, my grandmother's kitchen tools. It is such a privilege to bring these passions together in this book, in the company of Kath and Omid.

*Natasha*

*af.*

Published in 2015 by Murdoch Books, an imprint of Allen & Unwin

Murdoch Books Australia
83 Alexander Street
Crows Nest NSW 2065
Phone: +61 (0) 2 8425 0100
Fax: +61 (0) 2 9906 2218
murdochbooks.com.au
info@murdochbooks.com.au

Murdoch Books UK
Erico House, 6th Floor
93-99 Upper Richmond Road
Putney, London SW15 2TG
Phone: +44 (0) 20 8785 5995
murdochbooks.co.uk
info@murdochbooks.co.uk

For Corporate Orders & Custom Publishing contact
Noel Hammond, National Business Development Manager, Murdoch Books Australia

Publisher: Corinne Roberts
Editorial Manager: Barbara McClenahan
Design Manager: Hugh Ford
Food styling and photography: Omid Jaffari
Set styling and photography: Natasha Blankfield
Designer: Katy Wall
Additional design: Natasha Blankfield
Editors: Susie Ashworth and Ariana Klepac
Food Editor: Grace Campbell
Production Manager: Mary Bjelobrk

A cataloguing-in-publication entry is available from the catalogue of the National Library of Australia at nla.gov.au.

ISBN 978 1 76011 002 4 Australia
ISBN 978 1 74336 320 1 UK

A catalogue record for this book is available from the British Library.

Colour reproduction by Splitting Image Colour Studio Pty Ltd, Clayton, Victoria
Printed by Hang Tai Printing Company Limited, China

IMPORTANT: Those who might be at risk from the effects of salmonella poisoning (the elderly, pregnant women, young children and those suffering from immune deficiency diseases) should consult their doctor with any concerns about eating raw foods.

MEASURES GUIDE: We have used 20 ml (4 teaspoon) tablespoon measures. If you are using a 15 ml (3 teaspoon) tablespoon add an extra teaspoon of the ingredient for each tablespoon specified.